TEAM
HABITS

TEAM HABITS

How Small Actions
Lead to Extraordinary Results

CHARLIE GILKEY

NEW YORK

Hachette Go, an imprint of Hachette Books
Hachette Book Group
1290 Avenue of the Americas
New York, NY 10104
HachetteGo.com
Facebook.com/HachetteGo
Instagram.com/HachetteGo

First Edition: August 2023

Hachette Books is a division of Hachette Book Group, Inc.

The Hachette Go and Hachette Books name and logos are trademarks of Hachette Book Group, Inc.

The Hachette Speakers Bureau provides a wide range of authors for speaking events. To find out more, visit www.hachettespeakersbureau.com or call (866) 376-6591.

Hachette Go books may be purchased in bulk for business, educational, or promotional use. For information, please contact your local bookseller or email the Hachette Book Group Special Markets Department at Special.Markets@hbgusa.com.

The publisher is not responsible for websites (or their content) that are not owned by the publisher.

Print book interior design by Linda Mark

Library of Congress Cataloging-in-Publication Data
Name: Gilkey, Charlie, author.
Title: Team habits: how small actions lead to extraordinary results / Charlie Gilkey.
Description: First edition. | New York: Hachette Go, 2023. | Includes bibliographical references and index.
Identifiers: LCCN 2022057214 | ISBN 9780306828331 (hardcover) | ISBN 9780306828348 (trade paperback) | ISBN 9780306828355 (ebook)
Subjects: LCSH: Teams in the workplace. | Leadership. | Communication in management.
Classification: LCC HD66 .G548 2023 | DDC 658.4/022—dc23/eng/20230119
LC record available at https://lccn.loc.gov/2022057214

ISBNs: 9780306828331 (hardcover); 9780306828355 (ebook)

Printed in the United States of America

LSC-C

Printing 1, 2023

CONTENTS

To Angela Wheeler, the most unwavering,
amazing teammate I have ever belonged with.

ONE · WE NEED BETTER TEAM HABITS NOW MORE THAN EVER

If you do not change direction,
you may end up where you are heading.

—LAO TZU

"I'm at my wits' end, Charlie! This project ended up back on my lap, even though two months ago, I told the team I was concerned that this would happen, and they were, too. Now I can't get to my real strategic work because I'm doing their work!"

"Oof, it sucks when you see the train coming and you still get hit by it."

"Right?! I can't figure out why this keeps happening. Why can't they just . . . do it?"

"They're all smart, experienced, and committed to the goal, right?"

"Yes. That's what makes this so hard!"

"Okay, so what we're dealing with here is a broken printer."

"Huh? What's a broken printer have to do with this?"

□   □   □

2 - TEAM HABITS

"I'm so burned out, Charlie! I spend all day answering questions, approving things that don't need approval, and reminding people what we talked about. The only way I'm keeping my job is that I get up three hours earlier to do my work before the team gets online."

"That's rough. Is this a recent thing, or has it been going on for a while?"

"I've been here two years, and it was this way when I got here. No matter how many conversations I have, they roll back in the next day with more questions."

"Got it. What we're dealing with here is a broken printer."

"Uh . . . I don't think you understand. We work remotely, and this has nothing to do with printers."

□   □   □

"I can't get my best work done, Charlie! As soon as I get to work, I'm in meetings most of the day, and when I'm out of meetings, I have to catch up on Slack threads to make sure I haven't missed anything."

"Yeah, it's hard to do any of your best or deep work when your schedule looks like Swiss cheese. I'm curious: Is it this way just for you or for others struggling with the same thing?"

"It's all of us! It seems like every other meeting or Slack thread, we talk about how many meetings we have or how we're behind on Slack."

"Hmm. Seems like we're dealing with a broken printer, then."

"You're such a Boomer, my dude. Nobody prints stuff anymore."

□   □   □

I have conversations like the ones above every day with clients, readers, and students. Yes, I do get teased about being a Boomer even though I'm on the threshold between Gen X and Millennial, and yes, I do find it hilarious.

And I do end up unpacking what I mean by "broken printer." Every team has them—including yours. It's probably why you picked up this book. So what's a broken printer?

Every organization I've ever worked at or consulted with has had a literal broken printer that everyone knows about but no one fixes. You know the one.

It's the printer that leaves a streak down the page, which is fine for a team meeting agenda but not when it's time to provide a printout for the Big Boss or a customer.

Or the printer that randomly eats paper or needs the special kind of paper that never seems to be in stock.

Or the one that's downstairs in the office manager's office, but she's always in meetings and by the time she's out, the team has to figure out which printout belongs to who.

Or the one that has a passcode people can never remember or that always needs to be reprogrammed.

Or the one sitting on someone's desk, in a closet, or on the unused extra chair in the corner of the conference room.

There's *always* a broken printer. It may not seem like a broken printer is a big deal until you look at the downstream effects. Because the printer's broken:

- Teammates are rushed and frazzled in front of the Big Boss or customer because they had to scramble to reprint everything after the printer left that 😣 streak.
- The paper budget for the office is always over because of that special kind of paper.
- The IT department (aka Liz) has to stop what they're doing to fix the printer seven times a week, costing them—and everyone else—time.
- People are distracted during meetings because they're looking at agendas and docs on devices rather than printed agendas and review copies. Whatever's being discussed has to compete with notifications, emails, and inadequate screen sizes.

- Someone always has to roll another chair into the conference room, adding another five minutes of work before the meeting or creating a "wait for Taylor to get settled in" awkward start to the meeting.

Each small downstream effect from the broken printer may seem insignificant. But when multiplied by how frequently these small effects occur, they lead to massive waste, inefficiency, and demoralization.

The Progress Principle by Steven Kramer and Teresa Amabile[1] showed that the frequency of small setbacks and frustrations plays an outsized role in a team's morale and engagement. The grumbling, exasperation, and "keep it together before I lose my shit" moments that are happening because of the broken printer become part of the emotional labor of your daily work.

But here's the deal: **For most teams, it would cost less than $500 to replace the printer.** It might even just be a matter of noticing the printer in the corner and getting rid of it. Thousands of dollars in wasted team hours and daily #FML moments are hinging on a $500 decision or fifteen-minute action.

The broken printer isn't a big deal; what it causes and why it's not being addressed are *huge* deals. We can call a meeting that costs the organization twice what replacing a printer would without thinking about it, but the broken printer is an intractable problem?

Interesting.

The broken printer is a symptom of root-cause team dynamics that we'll discuss shortly, but in case your work hasn't been disrupted by a broken printer, don't worry—it's not *really* about printers.

SOMETIMES IT'S NOT A PRINTER

I've been talking about *actual* printers because the pattern of broken printers is near ubiquitous, tangible, and easy to understand for those of us who've been in the workforce for a while, which makes the broken printer a perfect shorthand for all those small and fixable breaks in the ways we work with each other.

But plenty of broken printers aren't literally printers. For instance, one of my executive coaching clients recently found out that one of her organization's mental health therapists hadn't been able to see her patients for the previous three months because she was missing an $8 computer cord.

Not even considering the many thousands of dollars my client's organization had spent on the therapist's salary, the therapist wasn't serving her patients during the COVID-19 pandemic—exactly when many of them were struggling with their mental health. The therapist's manager had known she needed a cord for three months, as had the IT department. It was only during a meeting called because of inaccurate financial reporting that this came up.

Yes, an $8 cord. Rest assured that my client made sure the therapist had her cord the day we talked about it.

A broken printer doesn't even have to be a physical issue. Take the CC Thread from Hell. Untold hours of many people's days are spent reading email CC threads trying to figure out how—or whether—they're relevant. The same pattern has moved to group chat tools such as Slack with overmentioning groups and channel bombing. Most of us know it's a problem, but no one is doing anything to fix it.

Or maybe your broken printer is the "choose your own adventure" way that teammates give each other tasks: Some use email, some text, some Slack; others call meetings; and a rare few actually task people in the team task management app. People need to look in seven different places for incoming tasks and hope they catch them all.

Or maybe it's requesting permissions on collaborative documents several times a day. It's not clicking the button to request permissions that's the biggest annoyance. It's being stuck while waiting for thirty minutes, a few hours, or until the next day for the document owner to come back around. And let's not even get started about how many times we've been left hanging with permission fails when someone goes on vacation.

Just as the physical broken printer doesn't have to remain broken, these ways of working with each other—what I'll call *workways*—are all fixable.

WHAT ARE WORKWAYS?

Our workways are determined by a mix of our team habits, organizational policies, technology, regulatory compliance, and org structure. Each of these creates a system, and, as in any system, changes or effects in one of them can change or create effects in other parts. These workways can support our work if they're healthy, or they can get in the way if they're broken—and not addressing broken workways is a choice.

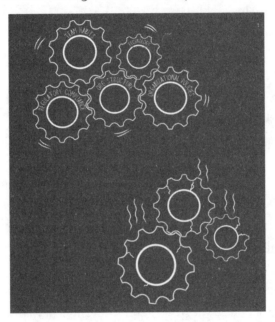

For this book, I will be focusing on the subset of workways around team habits because they're the universal subset of workways that we all participate in and can change. Just as we have personal habits that may be good or bad, every team has habits that support the work or get in the way. And just as with personal habits, it's possible to identify the bad ones and shift them into something more positive.

I want to make this point clear: **No matter your role in the company, you have the power to change your team's habits.** And improving team habits can be a lever to make changes in other, more intractable workways.

We can all change team habits, *and* that doesn't mean we all have the same power to do so or that the weight of other workways won't be working against us. Many of us work in rigid hierarchies or in workplaces that are riddled with thorny group dynamics. Many of us are from backgrounds that mean we'll be fighting implicit biases within our organization or the greater culture. Many of us are in industries with heavily ingrained norms and structural limitations.

That said, we can spend time grimacing and complaining about things that we can't change or are not well positioned to change while overlooking the stuff we *can* change right in front of us. Railing against macro workways like your industry's norms doesn't do much to solve the way those norms influence your team habits. Since you're going to have team habits regardless of what's happening in your industry, you're better off acknowledging those industry norms and getting busy with changing your team habits *today, where you are.*

In a world where most leadership, teamwork, and change management books focus on lofty ideas, the future of work, and grand strategies, I'm proposing something simple and mundane: If you want your team to work better, focus on your team habits.

WHY START WITH TEAMS?

You'll no doubt notice that I've started this book talking not about people but about broken printers and team habits. It may seem counterintuitive that a book about building better teams doesn't start with people, but it's by no means an accident. Countless books focus on changing people to make better teams—whether that's improving the manager or empowering individual contributors or upskilling leaders—but the usual result is that the team and organization basically stay the same.

Teams are made up of people, though, so it's helpful to understand that most people

- Are intrinsically goal-oriented. That doesn't mean that we're necessarily ambitious, but our basic wiring is such that we seek to avoid pains and secure gains.

- Want to be liked and in good relationships with other people. Again, basic human wiring here; we're inherently a cooperative species.
- Enjoy getting stuff done. While this may seem to be the same thing as being goal-oriented, it's not. This one's more about our emotional states vis-à-vis task completion versus our mental states around goal orientation.

No one wakes up in the morning and says, "You know what? I'm going to screw over my team today and not get anything done." No one except sociopaths or someone who's been pushed over an edge, that is.

That leaves us with a mystery. If people are inherently goal-oriented, relationship-minded, and completion-motivated, working in teams should be much smoother and easier than most people report. Furthermore, if we address team problems as if they are people problems, we're starting with the assumption that at least one of the members of the team doesn't have basic human wiring.

If teams are working well or poorly, it's not really about the people in the team. It's about how they're working together. Teams are the fundamental value-creation unit of businesses and organizations. Individuals alone don't create value—it's the interactions of individuals with each other that create value, whether that value is results, innovation, revenue, goods, services, or experiences. The value creation of teams is what differentiates the Disney World experience from a lone busker on a street corner wearing a Mickey Mouse suit.

But, to me, the most important reason to focus on teams is this:

TEAMS ARE WHERE WE EXPERIENCE BELONGING

We've all heard the quip that people don't leave bad companies, they leave bad managers. There's some truth to it, but I think it misses the mark because it places the emphasis on the manager rather than on the team habits that allow bad managers to remain in power.

What it rightly points out is that people quit or stay because of the people they interact with daily. No matter the size of the organization, most of us spend 80 percent of our work time with the same four to eight people. These people are our true team, regardless of what the org chart says.

And it's in this team that we experience belonging—or the opposite. Most of us have had the experience of sticking through a bad work experience because of our team; if it weren't for them, we would've flipped the table and walked out a long time ago. We've also experienced the feeling of having the good work we're doing soured by a frustrating or toxic environment created by a poorly functioning team.

That's the power of teams.

With a strong team, we have an incredible amount of rapport, influence, and can-do attitude. If our meetings suck, we can change them. If we want to come up with a different way of talking about goals, we can do it. If we want to cover for each other, we can come together and figure out how.

And if we make our team's work life better, we make 80 percent of our work life better. When our team's life becomes better, our sense of belonging goes up, making us even more invested in sticking with the team and making things better.

That's the power of teams, too.

Throughout this book, when you read something that makes you want to shake your fist at all the things you can't change at work, remember that what we're talking about is improving your team's belonging and performance, not the entire organization's.

But it turns out that focusing on your team is often the best way to change the organization.

HOW 3 PERCENT SHIFTS THE CULTURE

We think that change comes from the top, but the reality is that two-thirds of all top-down organizational change projects fail.[2]

Top-down change projects are tricky undertakings, in part because getting groups of people to change behavior is less about inspiring them with visionary ideas than about translating those ideas into everyday habits that everyone participates in.

But it turns out that a relatively small percentage of a culture or organization—as small as 3 percent—can shift the rest of the culture or organization they belong to. Nassim Nicholas Taleb writes convincingly about this in his book *Skin in the Game*,[3] where he suggests that within a complex system, it takes only "three or four percent of the total population, for the entire population to have to submit to their preferences."

While we might not live in a truly meritocratic culture, our culture does value what works. When one team starts outshining other teams, people at all levels of the organization take notice. The team's peers notice; studies suggest that employees learn more from their fellow employees than from higher-ups or managers.[4] And the better that team performs, the more likely it is that the organization's managers and leaders will start trying to figure out what's working.

Sure, they'll start by focusing on the *people* of the team and attributing their success to them. But, as I've argued above, it's not about the people per se. It's about their habits.

Organizational culture can be defined as a shared set of values, goals, attitudes, and practices that make up an organization. Team habits are the practical component of culture; while values, goals, and attitudes are important, when it comes down to it, *what we do as a collective is who we are as a collective.*

Changing our habits can be an incredible lever for changing our organizational culture. Continuing with our existing habits reinforces our current culture. If you don't like your organization's culture, then you have to change its habits.

To continue running the same habits is only to reinforce the culture. The single best way to shift your organization is to shift your team. And the single best way to keep your team together is to show that it's not the members of the team as much as it is the team habits—and *those* can be replicated across the organization fairly quickly and with minimal heartbreak and personnel disruption.

The power is in your hands.

Improve your team's habits. Get some points on the company scoreboard. Invite people from outside your team to join a project to see how it's done. Get yourself invited to join their projects to help them do them better.

That's how you can change your organization, if that's what you're out to do. It's not quick, it's not a one-time deal, and it's not easy.

USE MY HARD-WON LESSONS

Before we get into the nuts and bolts of team habits and how to change them, you might be wondering who exactly I am and what I know about effective teams.

I've been involved in the art and craft of leadership for the last three and a half decades, getting an early start in the Boy Scouts leadership program and growing up in an Army family. I was leading and teaching when I was a teenager and haven't strayed far from it since, despite my efforts to the contrary.

My most formative and intense leadership experiences came from my service with the US Army and Army National Guard in the 2000s. I deployed in support of Operation Iraqi Freedom as a transportation platoon leader and, while deployed, was reassigned to higher headquarters as the battalion plans officer, battle captain, and primary investigator during after-action reviews for convoys that were ambushed or experienced significant events such as accidents.

In the first two roles, I spent a lot of time ensuring that convoys were prepared and ran smoothly. In the latter role, I detailed what had gone wrong so that I could formulate and relay tactics, techniques, and procedures (TTPs) that were then spread throughout the theater of operation. One of the convoy ambushes I investigated was the most complex convoy ambush of Operation Iraqi Freedom.[5]

Once I redeployed, I was executive officer (second in charge) of my unit, which became the fastest unit to finish its redeployment and resume stateside operations. During this time, I also took on a special duty assignment to train joint and international units on how to conduct tactical convoy operations, using my in-theater experience and TTP knowledge. After this assignment, I was given company command of a redeploying unit and subsequently beat the redeployment record I had helped achieve in my previous unit.

Just as significant as what my units were achieving was what they were going through at the time. The commander of the unit I deployed with was relieved while in theater, and the unit I took command of state-side also had its commander relieved. Thus, in the mix of high-tempo operations and transitions, I was also in the midst of rebuilding leadership teams and company cultures.

It was an intense six years of learning to fix the plane while flying it.

Through it all, I kept noticing a pattern: **The most successful leaders and units were the ones that focused on what many would see as the minutiae.**

While I was fortunate to have great sergeants and junior officers in my units, some of the most important things I did were the simplest: I ensured that troops got paid on time, that their administrative requests were attended to, that I didn't step into my sergeants' lane (and that my officers didn't, either), and that I did my job of interacting with our battalion and higher headquarters so my troops could stay focused on their mission with as little interference from higher headquarters as possible. I also learned the cost of leaders hoarding information and micromanaging everything.

Toward the end of my military career, I began blogging and teaching about productivity, planning, leadership, and entrepreneurship at Productive Flourishing. What started as a way to explore my personal challenges as I worked toward completing my PhD in philosophy while managing my Army career and life turned into a coaching and education business. My graduate work in ethics, sociopolitical philosophy, and human rights immersed me in what creates the conditions for personal and social thriving and, apparently, gave my approach to the topics a richer spin for a lot of people.

Along the way, people started asking me to advise them on their leadership challenges. I've been an executive and business coach since 2009, with more and more of my work skewing toward executive coaching, strategy execution consulting, and workplace consulting for scale-ups and organizations since 2014.

I'm also actively engaged in the nonprofit and philanthropic communities, serving on executive committees of organizations that are solving root-cause challenges such as education inequities. Board and nonprofit service keeps me fluent in collaborative leadership and is a great complement to the directive leadership contexts of military service and entrepreneurship.

Today, my team at Productive Flourishing ranges from ten to thirty people, depending on how you count and the projects we're working on, so I stay in the mix of leading and managing a continually evolving team. Counterintuitively, leading Team PF is far more challenging than any of my previous leadership experiences, even including leading tactical convoy operations. Over the past fourteen years, I've had ample time to practice, experiment, fail, and iterate with my own team.

I want to be explicit that I'm not trying to guide the re-creation of the militaristic/hierarchical species of organizations that were seminal for me. Ironically, it was the defects of those kinds of organizations that led me to explore how to transform them.

You should've seen the horror and response of my sergeants when I discussed having upward and/or 360-degree feedback for *all of us* so that we could become better leaders—this was decades before Kim Scott's *Radical Candor.*[6] I was a lieutenant at the time, so I knew to pick my battles, but the inquiries I took away from that experience led to the way we do "performance reviews" at Productive Flourishing (which include the owners being in the support/hot seat) and how I think about 360-degree feedback for my executive clients.

I share the above not to brag but to give you a sense of what grounds the perspectives I'll be sharing in the book. The different contexts and sheer volume of cases I've seen throughout the decades continue to show the same patterns: **The delight of teamwork is in small day-to-day interactions that lead to wins and belonging.** Of course, the devils are there, too, in the broken printers and small broken promises we experience daily.

ACCEPT THE UNWANTED GIFTS OF VUCA AND COVID-19

The truth is, we've all gone through a crash course in change management over the past few years. That's one of the gifts of our current VUCA environment and COVID-19.

VUCA is an acronym that emerged from military education and theory in the '90s. While military strategists framed it in the context of military scenarios, they were describing the state of the world that was emerging quickly.

The four elements of VUCA are volatility, uncertainty, complexity, and ambiguity.

It seeped into civilian leadership and strategic conversations in the 2000s as the Internet and rapid pace of change caused by technology made the world even more VUCA. The insight and enduring power of the VUCA paradigm are that leading and working in a VUCA environment are fundamentally different than leading and working in a "stable" environment. The classic principles of leadership, management, and work that we've read and been taught either don't work or need to be approached dramatically differently.

Understanding the VUCA paradigm also helps us embrace the dynamism of team habits.

- What works this quarter may not survive into the next (volatility).
- Our business or organizational models are likely to change, but we don't know how or when (uncertainty).
- Small changes in one aspect of our team or organization will create changes elsewhere (complexity).
- What we thought was signal may be noise, and vice versa (ambiguity).

We thus have to live in the tension of doing the best we can to create consistency, clarity, simplicity, and coherence—the opposite of VUCA— all the while knowing that VUCA is the gravity of the work world we live in. And, for those of us who are possibilitarians, the VUCA environment provides a lot of opportunity to experiment with, change, and address workways that weren't working before VUCA times and aren't now, either.

As if the VUCA world we live in wasn't enough, COVID-19 changed the world of work irrevocably.

COVID-19 shredded almost all our existing habits. We went from remote working being something some companies were trying to the default way many of us worked. People who hated virtual meetings had no option but to show up for them. Social processors who normally found outlets with coworkers during coffee breaks suddenly had to figure out how to ask for brainstorming or sound-boarding sessions. Many of us who had learned to work without our kids, partners, and pets around found that working from home *with them* was more work than we were being paid to do. And a host of bonding activities based on physical proximity were taken away. Many of us still haven't found substitutes.

Still, there are three major upshots of the massive disruption to workplaces that COVID-19 caused:

1. It exposed a lot of habits that had been invisible. As I'll show, good team habits have a way of becoming invisible and bad team habits come to be accepted as normal. We couldn't "see" them until we were removed from our normal work context, in much the same way that we can't see our own homes until we come back from traveling.

2. We didn't feel that we had an option to change them before. But because so many of our team habits were contingent on working a certain way that we no longer could, the disruption created both the opening for change and the necessity for it.

3. We learned that, yes, we can change our existing team habits and create new team habits. Team habits and workways weren't something we merely had to participate in but rather were ways of working with each other that *we* created and maintained. That means we could re-create them as well as merely participate in them.

Turns out you don't need a pandemic to create a better new normal—it just did the work of beating inertia for us.

Since we have to create a new normal, how can we make a better new normal? After all, we're going to be creating new team habits anyway, so why not think about what habits will create more belonging and better performance?

I've been posing the following question to my clients, my team, and the nonprofits I'm engaged with.

WHAT ARE YOU GOING TO DO ABOUT YOUR BROKEN PRINTERS?

Perhaps you just said, "Charlie, with everything going on, we don't have time to work on the small things. The broken printers just aren't a priority."

Fair enough. Are you willing to look your teammates in the eye and say that out loud, though? Because you're really saying, "Fixing the things that would enable us all to work better together and be happier at work really isn't a priority."

Actually, don't worry about saying it out loud—your actions already are.

As I write this in 2022, many of us have lost the zeal for change that we might have had two years ago. We've adapted, pivoted, and readjusted ourselves into burnout, and now we're looking for some constancy in a world that's been extra VUCA lately.

At the same time, there are still plenty of broken printers sitting around. Some may have been there prior to the big shift; others were likely caused by it. The question is not whether they're there but whether you and your teammates are ready to fix them.

There are two inevitabilities when it comes to team habits: You're already participating in them, and they will eventually change—though not necessarily for the better. As management consultant Peter Drucker said, though, "The only things that evolve by themselves in an organization are disorder, friction, and malperformance." If positive change were automatic, we wouldn't have broken printers and CC Threads from Hell.

Changing broken team habits requires time and focus. **But if the prospect is daunting, remember that—one way or another—you're going to be participating in team habits, and change is inevitable.** I hope you'll choose to participate in them with intention and a goal to make things better.

Or maybe you've said, "Charlie, I'm not a manager or senior leader. The broken printer makes me crazy, but what can I possibly do about it?"

I want us to abandon the assumption that change management is a concern only for managers, senior leaders, and the consultants they hire to facilitate it. I want us to democratize change management in the same way that lean thinking democratized manufacturing and operations; one of the key insights from the lean paradigm is that the best ideas often come from the people closest to the work.

No matter your role, you're closest to your work and how your team works. A lot that happens in your team, like Vegas, can stay in your team and not require outside approval or resources. Most of the changes we'll discuss in this book can be made without the permission of anyone but the people on your team. Your team already has habits; we're going to discuss making changes and substitutions to what you're already doing.

Being the person who's closest to your work and how your team works gives you a major responsibility. **You're either participating in broken team habits or you're working to change them.**

From here on out, you can't just go to work anymore. Every day you go to work, you now have to ask whether your team's habits support your team's performance and belonging. If they do, build on them. If they don't, fix them.

You're already involved, anyway.

The real problem is that making these kinds of team changes has been relegated to managers and leaders, and there's just not enough decision-making and management bandwidth to go around. But what if we change that paradigm and make doing this work as simple and expected as calling a meeting?

Over the last twenty years of leading Army units, building teams, coaching executives and entrepreneurs, and serving on nonprofit boards,

I've seen what happens when teams improve their habits and team members own their relationship with each other. I've seen what happens when leaders remove barriers and stop forcing change from the top down, instead bringing everyone into the process. **Spoiler alert: Belonging and retention improve, teams start performing better, and people actually want to show up to work with each other.**

Turns out, it doesn't have to be the case that Gallup's employee disengagement statistics are so consistently alarming. The reason people are so disengaged isn't because of their innate dissatisfaction with work; it's because organizations are fine with letting broken printers stay broken.

What we will be exploring throughout this book is how fixing broken printers and improving team habits can be woven into the myriad other decisions and conversations your team is *already* having.

Here's what I want you to think about.

- If you're a senior leader: How many broken printers are sitting around your organization? What's it costing you in performance and morale? Why do they remain broken?
- If you're a manager or team leader: What's keeping you from fixing your team's broken printers?
- If you're an individual contributor: How have you engaged with your team and manager to fix the broken printers you struggle with every day?

If you're not a mix of constructively frustrated and inspired to fix the broken printers that you, your team, and your organization struggle with every day, please put this book down. It won't be for you.

If you're a leader or manager and have checked out on making things better for your team, please put down any sense of entitlement and privilege about being in your position, too, as you're no longer earning them.

If your team's consensus is that you're not ready to engage with your team habits, great! You can all stay focused on what matters more to you, understanding that your inevitable conversations about team habits are venting sessions more than problem-solving conversations.

But if you're ready to engage with your team habits and improve your, your team's, and your organization's lives and work, let's not wait for another pandemic, massive external shift, or internal crisis to get after it. It's much easier to play with team habits outside a crisis than in one.

HOW TO READ THIS BOOK

Since you're now better acquainted with both my philosophical and military background, you'll perhaps appreciate that I'm not going to leave you wondering where we're going and why. I'm going to use the well-worn Army framework of "Tell 'em what you're going to tell 'em, tell 'em, then tell 'em what you told 'em." That's a communication team habit that's not broken, so I'm not going to fix it.

This book is divided into three parts.

- **Part 1:** This part (which includes this chapter) contains the introduction to and overview of team habits. It will orient you to what team habits are, explain how they're the key to working better together, and acquaint you with the different categories of team habits. This part will also include a quick Team Habits Audit that will help you diagnose which category to start with.
- **Part 2:** In this part, we'll discuss each category of team habits on its own. I'll share patterns and habits that you can try in your team. Not every team habit suggestion will fit your team perfectly, and that's okay—my broader goal is to be close enough that you can adapt it to fit your team's context.
- **Part 3:** This part explains how to build a plan to change your team habits. Because team habits are shared agreements, it will start with the political and social dimensions of making change happen. It will then move into how to make a plan and, finally, how to adapt once reality inevitably changes your plan.

Along the way, I'll be sharing various worksheets, tools, and resources. You can find a complete list of those at teamhabitsbook.com/resources.

You'll also find sidebars throughout the book that explain common organizational frameworks. These are meant to provide a simple overview to explain the concept and give everyone on the team—individual contributors, managers, and leadership—the same tools and language for talking about team habit change.

Oh, and there's a glossary in the back for all the "Charlie-isms" that you'll encounter as we go.

The only right way to read this book is the way that works best for you. I hope it stays on your shelf and you return to it as you need to, which means you'll probably engage with it differently each time. The book's structure gives you many ways to explore and use it, but there are four logical pathways:

1. Read the whole book front to back, and then start applying it.
2. Read Part 1 to get what you need, do the audit, read more about the category you're most called to work on, and then jump to Part 3 to start making your plan and working the plan.
3. Jump right to Part 3 because you already know which category of team habits you want to start with. If you're the expresso type, you can't go wrong with choosing Belonging, Decision-Making, or Meetings as the category to work on.
4. A variation of 2: you go back, read about the next category you're called to work on, and then start making your plan and putting it to work.

WHO THIS BOOK IS FOR

This book is not just for managers or senior leaders. **In fact, my goal is to democratize the idea of who gets to make change within an organization.**

Individual Contributor

As an individual contributor, you'll approach change differently than the Big Boss, who can just walk in and make changes with a snap of their fingers. My goal is to teach you how to become a good project champion and collaborator and give you the tools to start having discussions about habits within your own team. Share this book with your teammates and manager.

Manager

As a manager, you have more innate power within the organization to change things, but you're still probably only in charge of one team within the larger organizational culture. You can fix some bad team habits but not all of them. My goal is to help you audit which team habits are the biggest issue and give you the tools to see team habit change sprints through.

Senior Leader

This book will show you a different way to understand what's going on in your organization. It will give you a more granular view of why things do and don't work well and hopefully open your eyes to problem areas. After all, there typically aren't any broken printers in the senior executive's office. Your impulse while reading this book may be to jump in and clean up a whole mess of broken printers, but I want you to tamp down the urge to change too many things at once.

Why? **Because if you just unilaterally determine everything and drive the project yourself, you may have changed the organization, but you've created a team habit that relies on your will to change future team habits.**

Remember that you're probably too far removed from the actual work that's going on to choose the most effective solutions. My goal with this book is to help you understand *how* your organization makes changes in team habits and create a lingua franca around how team members at every level of your organization can approach change management.

For Every Teammate

As much as this book is about work, it's even more about relationships: the relationship you have to your work and the relationships you have with your teammates. The same questions that you find in books on personal relationships are analogous to the questions we ask ourselves about work and our teammates. (Are they the one? Can I trust them? How can we get along better? How can we create more positive shared experiences and meaning?)

As with working on relationships, any work you do to make work better will not be wasted time. The efforts you make to work better together with your team will likely transcend any work relationship you have with your teammates.

How would you feel if you knew a teammate was working to make your day-to-day work life better? To help you feel that you belong and matter? To trust that you've got it? To celebrate your contributions, respect your counsel, and have your back without your asking for it?

We can all be that teammate, whether we're individual contributors, managers, or senior leaders. The rest of this book will show you how.

CHAPTER 1 TAKEAWAYS

- Every team is hampered by small and fixable breaks in the way team members work with each other (broken printers).
- Just as we have personal habits that may be good or bad, every team has habits that support the work or get in the way. And just as with personal habits, it's possible to identify the bad ones and shift them into something more positive.
- If teams are working well or poorly, it's not really about the people in the team. It's about how they're working together.
- Team habits exist whether or not we acknowledge them. You're either participating in broken team habits or you're working to change them.
- No matter your role in your company, you have the ability to change your team's habits.

TWO # WE LIVE AND BREATHE TEAM HABITS

If you are going to achieve excellence in big things,
you develop the habit in little matters.

—GENERAL COLIN POWELL

A few years ago, I was working with a speaking coach. The first couple of sessions were originally frustrating for me because so little time was spent on my content, structure, and ideas. Rather than looking at my speeches, my coach was focused on the mechanics of how I speak.

It turns out that a lot of the problems speakers have come down to our ineffective breathing. At one point during a session, my coach said, "Charlie, you're already breathing all day. What we're working on is *how* you breathe and ensuring the way that you're breathing is supporting your performance."

I knew she was right. It was the same message every sports coach, yoga instructor, spiritual teacher, and Army leader had shared with me in different ways. Something as simple as breathing intentionally can have profound effects on everything you do, and since you're already doing it, you may as well do it right (meaning in a way that supports you).

Team habits are how a team or organization breathes. The breathing is happening whether you notice it or not. Simply by being there and being a part of the team or organization, you're involved in this breathing process. As your team's work tempo changes, your team's habits will be stressed or relieved. As your team's composition or goals change, your team's habits may need to shift.

You've probably been through the process of replacing old personal habits with new ones. Maybe you decided to take up running, cut sugar out of your diet, start a meditation practice, or replace your evening social media scroll with reading a book. You probably experienced how easy it is to fall back on the inertia of old habits and how conscientiously you need to drill in your new habits through intentional repetition and consistency.

You might also have attempted to change your individual work habits to better support you. Maybe you scheduled focus blocks during your most productive times, batched and stacked tasks, or tried any number of the other personal effectiveness habits I talked about in my last book, *Start Finishing*[1]. If so, you might have run up against an even greater challenge, one that many people have asked me about since *Start Finishing* came out: You want to make habit changes in your personal work schedule but feel trapped working the way team culture dictates.

You're not alone. I've heard from everyone from individual contributors to senior leaders who feel stuck in their team habits. It doesn't have to be that way. In your team, **that small group of four to eight people who you spend 80 percent of your working time with, you have an incredible amount of influence.** Maybe you can't change the CC Thread from Hell that is so pervasive in your company culture, but you can eliminate it from your own team habits. And you can minimize its impact on how you all work.

MOVING MOUNTAINS IS HARD; MOVING STONES IS EASIER

When we build team habits, we're building them in the same way that we build habits for individuals. And, as with building or changing an individual habit, this sort of work doesn't happen overnight. Which means it can get discouraging.

We get habits to stick via consistent repetition and positive feedback loops. Our entrenched habits have both of these elements: consistent repetition (inertia) and positive feedback loops (low cognitive, emotional, and social labor via habituation). To roll out new habits, we need to repeat them to the point of collective habituation and amplify the positive feedback loops of better results and belonging.

A shift happens when we switch from individual action and choices to social action and choices. If I'm a solo worker and I change my schedule to work for me, there may be a few consequences, but it's mostly pretty straightforward. If I work in a team setting, changing my schedule requires negotiation, communication, consideration of other people's needs and availability, understanding of the precedents the change may set, and a whole litany of other considerations that are essentially social overhead (the ongoing or indirect social costs of operating or maintaining a team's or organization's way of being).

As individuals and groups, we'll exchange only lower cognitive, emotional, and social labor for something that most of us agree is better. Luckily, most of us agree that more winning and belonging are better and are willing to do the change work to get there.

As you're going about the work of changing team habits, it's insufficient to just talk about the *how*—you have to talk about the *why* of change. It doesn't have to be some grand company purpose; more everyday small wins, belonging, and ease are quite sufficient.

And it turns out that everyday small wins, belonging, and ease are things we can *all* participate in.

We have a bias in our society, especially in the business world, toward making sweeping changes. Is something not working well? Let's clear it out and start fresh.

But while the idea of tackling a big change sounds impressive, it's actually antithetical to the end goal of making lasting change. It's like wedging your crowbar underneath a massive boulder in the hopes of moving a mountain. At best, you end up frustrated when you have little to no progress to show after your efforts. At worst, you throw out your back and decide it's not worth it to try to make change in the future.

At the individual level, we're all familiar with the quick diet or quick habit change that ultimately doesn't stick. Unless you're one of the rare souls who can try a bunch of changes and be okay with them not sticking, the end result is that you'll become resistant or hardened to the next quick fix.

Because your team's habits are shared agreements and expectations, this same pattern plays out, but with more intensity. To change a habit, you're already negotiating with others to overcome inertia to try something new. Unless you're addressing a broken printer that everyone wants fixed—which is a great place to start, by the way—there's already an effort/reward calculation going on in your team. And quick-start change projects that don't stick only reinforce inertia and the feeling of "That's just how we do it here."

If you step away from the boulder and drop the crowbar, you'll start to notice that the mountain you're trying to move is actually made up of stones. Pick up a small one; you'll be surprised how much easier it is to carry and how much progress you can make moving one small stone at a time.

As you approach team habits, I want you to shift away from the big change management paradigm and focus on identifying the small things you can change more quickly. There are a few reasons for this.

Build Momentum Faster

If I had to guess, I would assume that you're already working at capacity. Your plate is full enough with the day-to-day responsibilities of your job even before you start tackling projects designed to improve your team's habits.

When you identify small projects to address, you'll begin to see change faster. Moving one stone—for example, eliminating the CC Thread from Hell—creates more bandwidth for you to address the next stone. And with each small stone you move, you and your teammates will see more progress and gain more momentum.

You'll also have an easier time telling the story of this project's success because there aren't so many moving parts involved. This serves both to energize your team and to prove to those outside your team that this work has value.

Work on a Human Timeline

The second reason to move stones instead of mountains is that the more you try to bite off, the longer the project will take and the harder it will be to maintain focus. As humans, we're primed to think in terms of months, which makes a month an ideal length of time for a team habit sprint. You can sustain energy on a project for a month because the short time span feels doable on a human timeline.

That said, some projects will take longer than others, and some organizations will work more quickly or slowly than others. In a large organization, a team habit sprint may take a quarter to see all the way through because things move a bit more slowly. But you shouldn't choose habits that will take a quarter to change. Instead, focus on a category and decide that over the course of a quarter, you'll focus on X habit this month, Y habit next month, and Z habit after that. Over the course of that quarter, you'll see the difference.

In the startup world, you can get a lot more done in a month. With a smaller team, you can focus your energy more fully. That's one of the advantages of being in a startup. The disadvantage, of course, is that you have to figure everything out on the fly.

Regardless of the size of your organization, picking smaller habit interventions that you can see through in a month will help you feel that sense of momentum.

Get Buy-in More Easily

Another reason to focus on shifting stones rather than moving mountains is that teams are self-correcting systems. The bigger the proposed change, the bigger the resistance you'll face, and the harder it will be to see lasting results. Moving small stones allows you to start identifying how the system will self-correct so you can address that specifically.

The truth is that changing a team habit may mean we all win in the long run—but in the short run, someone loses. Someone set up the original habit or benefits from it being that way. It could be that Bob just doesn't like databases, and so you have an entire department that runs on 243 different interlinked spreadsheets. It's inefficient, but because it's relatively functional, no one has tried to change it. Not to mention, you'll have to drag Bob kicking and screaming to the idea of using a database instead of the spreadsheet system he set up.

The mountain you need to move is transforming these spreadsheets into a database. But the first stone you need to carry is changing Bob's attitude toward databases. You need to teach Bob why your database solution is better and that he can get the same information without having to change anything—while the team's life will improve a lot.

In this scenario, Bob is the agent of system correction. If you try to overhaul the whole system at once, Bob might say, "You know what? It looks like you all don't have enough work right now because you have enough time to change all these spreadsheets." He'll pile your plate with busywork, and the next time you bring up spreadsheets, he'll stonewall your efforts.

Change one small spreadsheet that Bob isn't using much, though, and you'll be more likely to get buy-in. When he sees how well that project went, he'll probably buy in to the next one. By the time you're transforming all his spreadsheets into a database, Bob will have been brought slowly along to the point of view that this change is actually simpler than your old team habits.

Let Sleeping Dragons Lie, for Now

The last reason to focus on stones is that sometimes there are dragons under mountains.

Team habits aren't created in a vacuum; they're a reaction to the larger work culture of the organization. For instance, a team that has a terrible set of executives might learn to compensate by creating ineffi-cient habits that allow them to avoid taking things before the executives and dealing with the inevitable morass that creates. Their team habits may not be ideal, but they're in place because of this other fact that they can't control.

Shifting smaller stones lets you begin to illuminate the bigger prob-lem. You can say, "There's something here that needs to be addressed; what are we going to do about that?" You can start a productive dis-cussion. But if you start by moving the mountain, you might open a Pandora's box of problems that you can't simply put back.

THE EIGHT CATEGORIES OF TEAM HABITS

I've broken up the small instances of team habits into eight different cat-egories, but it's a bit of a simplification to insist on the distinctions among them. Many intermingle with each other. It can sometimes be hard to see whether a communication problem is leading to bad goal-setting, for example, or whether bad goal-setting is leading to a communication problem.

Still, working on team habits as part of a broader category bucket—instead of just grabbing a meeting habit, then a goal-setting habit, then a planning habit—helps you feel that you're making coherent progress in one area. And, of course, because these habits and categories are so interconnected, making a change in one area can result in a change in another area.

Defining categories gives teams an area in which to focus their efforts, but the category that a habit falls in doesn't matter so much as whether you're fixing the broken printer. If you focus on one category and create an anchor project around that, you'll start to move toward a better set of team habits overall.

I chose these categories because these are all things that keep coming up over and over again in conversations I have with people, whether on the personal productivity side or as it relates to their teams. These eight categories are relevant no matter what team you're on.

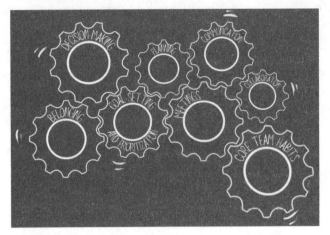

1. Belonging
2. Decision-Making
3. Goal-Setting and Prioritization
4. Planning
5. Communication
6. Collaboration
7. Meetings
8. Core Team Habits

These categories aren't necessarily listed in the order in which I recommend you tackle them (with the exception of belonging, which we'll talk about in a minute). After all, the broken printer that your team is struggling with most is unique.

One of these categories might feel like a natural starting point for your team. Maybe you all love your meetings, but you don't know what's supposed to happen once the meeting is over. That sounds like a collaboration problem. Maybe you all love your work, but you're getting tired of everything being so last minute all the time. That's a planning problem.

As you're deciding where to start, understand this:

The Problem You Start with Is Rarely the Root Problem— and That's Great

Let me give you an example.

I had a client who had a wonderful project manager with a highly performing team. When it came time for the project manager to be promoted into a different position, all of a sudden, the team began to struggle. On the surface, it looked like a problem with the project manager's promotion. It isn't unusual to see someone who has been promoted start to struggle with the responsibilities of their new leadership role, but this didn't seem to be the issue here.

Remember, issues with how teams work together are rarely *people* problems.

We started by working to help the project manager feel more belonging, calm, and ease in her role. We worked on communication and on her skills around meetings. After three or four months, we finally found that the real stress in her role was coming from team habits around goal-setting and prioritization.

Essentially, when this project manager was promoted, she became responsible for setting goals around team outcomes that she couldn't affect one way or another. This meant the team was now collaborating around goals that the project manager would never be able to push forward, which was creating immense frustration for everyone.

In the end, the problem we were trying to solve—that this newly promoted project manager was creating a toxic environment for her team—was at its core a problem of team alignment. The way her job was structured had created an unwinnable situation for the entire team.

Over the course of about a month's effort to change team habits around goal-setting, the change became clear. The team environment was healthier, and the team was able to focus better on the work that really mattered to them. We didn't need to change the project manager— we needed to change the team's habits around goal-setting and priorities.

As you start working on team habits, you'll eventually learn what the actual problem is, but hidden problems are hidden for a reason. And a lot of times, whether it's a sacred cow that no one wants to touch or whether it's just one of those unstated things that we don't ask about, that hidden problem isn't going to be your first answer.

Knowing this helps in a number of ways.

It Gets You Off the Starting Line

It's easy to be paralyzed by the paradox of choice. You don't need to decide ahead of time which habit is the right one to start with because when you start doing this work, you'll start to see how interconnected these habits are. If you change any one of them, you'll change all of them. They all touch each other.

Taking this approach also helps when it comes to getting consensus from the rest of your team on where to start. Even if everyone is thoroughly convinced that they're championing the right team habit to start with, starting work on any one bad team habit will get you closer to understanding what's at the core of all of them.

It Gives You Permission Not to Be 100 Percent Right

When you don't have to be right about where you start, it frees you from the worry that you need to get the diagnosis right before you start digging into the problem. Trust that you will eventually learn what the actual problem is, and understand that exploring the problem is simply part of the process.

The Army has a term called "collecting information by action," which is a sophisticated way of saying "Do stuff and see what happens." When it comes to changing team habits, if you're taking it seriously and your team is attuned to what's going on, you might choose wisely from the very beginning. But most of the time, the only way you can get the information you need about what's truly going on is to start taking action.

It Encourages You to Keep Going Deeper

Unless your team is extremely good at fishbone analyses or the Five Whys, usually the first problems they'll point out will be fairly high-level. For instance, meetings are a popular problem to start with. People want to fix the meeting culture, but part of the reason the meetings suck is that team habits around communication and collaboration suck. Because people don't know what's going on, or because roles and responsibilities aren't clear, you have to have constant meetings.

□□□ FRAMEWORK

FIVE WHYS AND FISHBONE ANALYSES

The Five Whys technique and fishbone analyses are great, simple tools to discover root causes.

The Five Whys technique, first laid out by Sakichi Toyoda, is a critical component of the Toyota Product System and Lean Thinking. To use the Five Whys technique, start by asking, "Why did this event/ situation occur?" When an answer to that question emerges, ask it again. Do it at least three more times.

While it's called the Five Whys exercise, you may need to ask "Why?" many more times to find the true root causes. You may also find that there are multiple, coequal reasons that something happened. Don't let the seeming linearity or the number five short-circuit what the technique is really about: going deep into what's causing what.

Once you become practiced with the Five Whys technique or notice that it's not going deep enough or is not comprehensive enough, try doing some fishbone analyses. Fishbone analyses do a much better job of showing clusters of root causes and grouping them into themes to work on. See our resources at teamhabitsbook.com/resources to learn more about how to do a fishbone analysis.

Similarly, belonging is an area where teams experience a lot of challenges, but it's rarely put on the table as something that needs to be fixed. On paper, tasks are being done and the work is happening. But if you take a wider view, you might see disengagement from your team in the form of high turnover or people doing just the work that's needed and no more. The symptom might be that, on the surface, your team doesn't seem to be collaborating well. But the root problem isn't team collaboration habits. It's belonging.

It Keeps You Curious

Finally, knowing that the problem you pick to start with likely isn't the root problem opens you up to being curious. I recommend that you approach team habit change scientifically: Start with a hypothesis and experiment rather than working through the problem with brute force. If you stay curious—rather than inflexibly implementing solutions—you'll keep paying enough attention to gather the information you need and make the changes you want to make.

Don't let yourself get caught up in the anxiety swirl of just *fixing something*. Instead, let yourself pause and be delightfully curious about what's really going on in your team. When you stay curious about the root cause of the problem, you can ask, "What else is at play here?" It allows you to go back to solving root causes rather than just making it about your own obsessions or finding easy scapegoats.

PICK YOUR STARTING POINT

All that said, where *should* you start?

It depends on the size and setup of your organization.

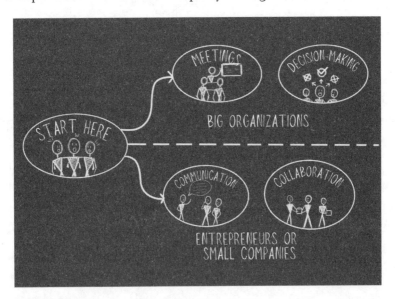

As a general guideline, I have three different go-tos, depending on the sector of work we're talking about. In my experience, working on your team habits in this order will get you the most wins the fastest.

If you're in a big organization, the team habits you'll probably need to work on the most are around belonging, then meetings, then decision-making. That's because larger organizations tend to have a much more dominant meeting culture. They also tend to have a byzantine decision-making structure in which, in order to get anything done, you need to know which of eighteen different people you might need to talk to. Or you might face a lot of political maneuvering and preconversations in order to move a decision forward.

On the entrepreneurial side, I still start with belonging and then suggest communication and collaboration. That's because entrepreneurs often are not great communicators, though they usually think they are. They're often still learning how to practice communicating to people outside their own head regarding what needs to happen, when it needs to happen, and so forth. This often creates a company culture that has plenty of heart and vision but has broken team habits around collaboration, delegation, and balance.

You might have noticed that I led both examples with belonging; it's also the first category we'll talk about in the book.

The reason I prioritize belonging for everyone is because it is the unaddressed foundation that everything else is built on. If you're part of a team that has high belonging, you can solve any other problem. Belonging team habits are the baseline for great performance. If your coworker is going out to get coffee and stops by your desk to say, "Hey, do you want me to get your normal oat-milk cappuccino?" The fact that they asked, and know your order, isn't about the coffee. It's about your relationship and the fact that you're in this together.

You can build a lot of healthy habits on that foundation. However, if you try to solve other problems but don't have high belonging, you're more likely to leave the core problem unaddressed.

Even if you are most excited to dig into a later category, like decision-making or collaboration, I encourage you to read the chapter on belonging before skipping ahead.

We're about ready to dive into the first team habit category: belonging. But first I want to offer a few final guideposts to help you on this journey. We'll discuss all of these in more detail in Chapter 3.

Use the IKEA Effect

Channel the joy of laying down your hex wrench, dusting off your hands, and admiring the IKEA bookshelves you just built from a kit. The IKEA effect refers to feeling more ownership over things we have a hand in, and team habit change is no exception. When you enroll your team in the process of changing your habits, the new habits are more likely to stick because *everyone* pitched in.

Team habit change isn't an individual task, and it's not about taking power or scoring wins. It's about building alignment.

Don't Fix Everything at Once

Pick the one (*one!*) category of team habits that you think will make the biggest difference and then spend some solid time improving how your team works in that area. Once you've spent some time fixing your most urgent broken printer, ask yourself if you still have major work to do in that category to get it to a level of acceptability or if you are ready to move on to the next thing.

Stay Open to the Outcome

Your team is a complex system, and changing that system will have unintended and surprising consequences. Because we'll be working on making small changes one at a time, you'll need to learn to celebrate fortunate surprises and say oops about unfortunate surprises.

If you do everything to avoid the small oopses, you'll also likely miss the fortunate surprises. Just remember that both wins and setbacks are happening with your small team; the change-by-change project stakes are low, and setbacks are ephemeral, but the mindset's end results of better belonging and performance are high and enduring.

Pick the Right-Sized Project

As I mentioned above, it's better to choose a smaller habit that you can change over the course of a one- or two-month sprint than to choose a habit that will take six months or more to change.

Be particularly mindful of this as you're getting started, when the tendency to bite off more than you can chew will be strong and you won't have enough experience with team habit change to judge how long it will take your team to work through a sprint.

Start with the Spark

Give your team the best chance at success by starting with the team habit that has the most spark for you or the one that touches on the thing that's most painful. It may be that you've got a broken printer that's driving you crazy or is something that everyone on the team has been complaining about for a while now.

When you start with the broken printer that's causing the most pain, the positive feedback loops for your team will be strong. If it's not clear which habit is the most painful, then work on the one that fires you up the most because then you'll have the positive feedback loop of making progress on something you really care about.

Take the Quiz

Whatever you think is the biggest problem your team faces, it might not be the same problem that another teammate thinks is the biggest. Defining the root problem is like the story of the blind men and the elephant in which each blind man is extrapolating the whole elephant from a single part: leg, trunk, or tail. Each person on your team will see the same root problem through their own lens of experience.

That's why I recommend taking the assessment at the end of this chapter. Just because you think your team's meeting habits suck doesn't mean the rest of your team would agree. Taking the assessment can help you gain clarity about what is most pressing. If possible, share the assessment with the rest of your teammates. Not only will this help you all clarify the real issue, but it will make it easier to get buy-in than if you just start doing your own thing.

BUILDING BETTER TEAM HABITS ISN'T ROCKET SCIENCE— IT'S ROCKET PRACTICE

The concept of team habits and the specific team habits we need to change aren't hard to understand. As the saying goes, they're not rocket science. That's the benefit, but it's also the downside.

On the one hand, "Treat everyone like a human" or "Set an agenda for your meetings" are pretty easy to say and understand. On the other hand, if it were that easy to do, wouldn't we already be doing it and seeing the results in our team?

Many healthy habits in our own lives are this way. We know that if we want to get in shape, we should pick a form of exercise and do it, but secretly, we want the solution to be more complicated than that.

If the answer is complex, we can let ourselves off the hook. If it's straightforward, then we don't have much of an excuse for not starting to build the habit. I see this often with my executive coaching clients. I encourage them to develop a practice of having regular five- to fifteen-minute conversations with their teams throughout the day (a practice described in the book *Touchpoints* by Douglas Conant and Mette Norgaard[2]) to help cultivate belonging among their teammates. These touchpoints could be as simple as checking in with a teammate about how their trip went, how a home remodeling project is going, or how their kid or pet is doing. Basically, showing interest in those parts of our lives that light us up outside work.

These quick one-on-one conversations—or even just a few Slack messages—can be a significant way to develop belonging and trust, yet too many leaders don't bother. When I suggest the practice to executive coaching clients, most are skeptical. "Really?" they ask. "That doesn't sound that complicated."

My answer is always the same: "It may sound simple, but are you doing it now? No? Then why not give it a shot and see what happens?"

It reminds me of the line from Chapter 53 of the *Tao Te Ching*:

> The Tao is broad and plain
> But people like the side paths

Team habit change is simple, but that doesn't mean it's easy. Especially not when you go looking for more complicated solutions rather than committing to the practice.

Those side paths are tempting because they give us an excuse for why we can't have better belonging, or stronger communication, or a more effective meeting culture. They give us an excuse to keep going with the flow instead of taking responsibility for fixing broken printers. If change is complicated, we're off the hook. But if it's actually simple?

Then it's on us if we decide to go with the status quo instead of pushing for a better work environment for ourselves and our teammates.

Understanding team habits and knowing what team habits you need to change aren't the hard parts; continually practicing until they become ingrained habits for your entire team *is*.

Changing team habits isn't rocket science. It's rocket *practice*.

That's why at the end of each team habit idea, you'll find a section titled "Rocket Practice" that will guide you through the steps of implementing that habit. The goal of rocket practice is to empower the team to point to the broad, plain road and simply ask, "Why aren't we walking down that instead of bushwhacking through the shrubbery?"

If a team habit change seems too simple to make a difference, it's probably just simple enough to work. Give it a shot and see what happens.

TEAM HABIT ASSESSMENT

The following assessment is meant to help you gauge which category of team habits is a good starting point for your team using familiar concepts and patterns. Note that each chapter will introduce new team habits, which may or may not directly relate to the questions used in this quiz. In other words, think of this quiz more as a tool and less as a table of contents.

BELONGING How your team creates belonging and meaning amongst members of the team	YES	NO
Company values are made clear and guide team action.		
Employees are valued as people not based on their output.		
Team members take the time to know the whole person at and outside work.		
Team members support one another in times of triumph and challenge.		
Team members know the work they do matters.		

DECISION-MAKING How your team makes decisions	YES	NO
Decision fatigue is reduced because decisions are made early and often.		

Team members know which decisions are theirs to make.
  1. The decisions they can make on their own without letting management know.
  2. The decisions they can make on their own but need to let management/leadership know they made them.
  3. The decisions they can't make and must defer to management/leadership.		

Team members are clear when a decision has been made to postpone or drop a project removing unnecessary project-level decisions.		

	YES	NO
Team members are clear when something has moved from an idea to a project requiring decisions and action.		
Team members are alerted when decisions have been made and why.		

GOAL-SETTING AND PRIORITIZATION
How your team sets goals and priorities

	YES	NO
The team is clear on their priorities and can identify the most important thing to work on each day.		
The team sets goals based on aspiration (**pull factors**) over avoidance (**push factors**).		
Company strategy informs work at all levels, creating a clear through-line between work done at individual, team, and company levels.		
The team understands how their short-term goals inform the company's long-term vision.		
The team reviews current commitments before taking on new projects to ensure they don't overcommit.		

PLANNING
How your team creates, distributes, and adjusts plans

	YES	NO
Team members plan their work at the daily, weekly, and monthly levels based on the team's monthly, quarterly, and annual goals.		
The team sets monthly, quarterly, and annual goals in conjunction with reviews from the same time perspectives.		
Projects have clear start and end dates.		
Team members are encouraged to schedule blocks of time for different types of work based on energy levels and to plot their tasks accordingly.		
Team members know how to respond when situations or circumstances change and adjust their plans and priorities accordingly.		

COMMUNICATION

How, what, and where your team communicates	YES	NO
Team members have access to information they need to do their job without needing to fill in gaps or search for what they need.		
Leaders communicate deadlines and priorities.		
Team members and leaders use clear and direct (and kind) language so nothing is left open to interpretation.		
Respect across the organization allows people to speak freely and openly.		
Teams use dedicated channels and tools for different communication needs.		

COLLABORATION

How your team moves objectives, projects, and tasks forward together	YES	NO
Teams have regular conversations to discuss how they are working as a team.		
Team members understand not just their roles and responsibilities but also those of everyone on the team.		
Boundaries are encouraged, expressed, held, and respected across the organization.		
The team knows how to effectively and fairly divide project tasks so each person has enough and no one is overwhelmed.		
The team knows how to and has permission to self-form project teams when necessary to get work done.		

MEETINGS

How your team prepares for, conducts, and follows up after meetings	YES	NO
Team meetings are well-run and constructive with an agenda, a facilitator, and the right people "in the room."		
Action items from meetings are captured, assigned, given due dates, and distributed after the meeting.		

	YES	NO
Team members feel that meetings support their work and are clear on how they can contribute.		
Teams work to keep to the agenda but allow for flexibility to adjust course when challenges or unexpected urgent situations arise.		
Teams limit the amount of meetings and plan in advance (as much as possible) so team members can plan their weeks without worrying about surprise meetings.		
CORE TEAM HABITS **How your team enables the effectiveness of individual members**	**YES**	**NO**
The team knows how each person works most effectively and actively looks for strategies to support those ways of working.		
Team members review their current individual commitments before saying yes to a new project to ensure that they are not overcommitting.		
When planning projects, team members deliberately create or indicate ways others can help them get things done.		
Each team member has a daily routine that supports them emotionally, creatively, and professionally.		
Team members divide their work into manageable chunks that keep them and the work of the team moving.		

CHAPTER 2 TAKEAWAYS

Team habits are how a team or organization breathes. The breathing is happening whether you notice it or not.

When changing team habits, start by moving stones rather than mountains. This helps you build momentum, get buy-in, and rack up early wins.

The eight categories of team habits are:

1. Belonging
2. Decision-Making
3. Goal-Setting and Prioritization
4. Planning
5. Communication
6. Collaboration
7. Meetings
8. Core Team Habits

It's more important to pick a habit and start working than to agonize over which habit is the exact right one to start with.

Changing team habits isn't rocket science—it's rocket *practice*. You'll find "Rocket Practice" sections throughout the book with tips and ideas for your team.

Take the Team Habit Assessment to find out where to start.

THREE **BELONGING**

*I dreamed about a culture of belonging. I still dream
that dream. I contemplate what our lives would be like
if we knew how to cultivate awareness, to live mindfully,
peacefully; if we learned habits of being that would bring us
closer together, that would help us build beloved community.*

— BELL HOOKS

The Boy Scout camp where I worked every summer as a teenager had a tradition: the Friday watermelon relay. Troops would send their best swimmers to the river with one simple task: Do a four-part, fifty-meter relay swim where one boy passed a watermelon off to the next.

There were two twists: We'd cake the watermelons with Crisco, and one boy had to control the watermelon at all times. Swimming with a full-sized watermelon was hard enough. When it was slathered in Crisco and one scout had to pass it to another, it was pure comic mayhem.

The Crisco watermelon relay is an apt metaphor for many collaborative projects. On the surface, they seem simple: I complete my part of the project and then hand it off to you. Except that somehow, the project becomes chaotic. Things are missed and fall through the cracks. The project keeps changing hands, becoming increasingly slippery along the way.

Some teams do better at managing Crisco watermelons than others. When they do, it's not because they have better meeting templates, communication tools, or decision-making frameworks.

It's because of *belonging*, the sense of shared meaning, safety, and membership in a group.

When projects become Crisco watermelons, a group with low belonging tends to pass blame and throw more people at the project. A team with high belonging stops to figure out *why* the watermelon keeps getting dropped. They understand that we're all tired and overcommitted, that we bring our lives outside work with us, and that we're distracted by meetings and technology. Belonging is what allows a team to take all that as a core assumption rather than stigmatizing it so they can figure out how best to support each other to move forward.

Belonging is what turns a group of people into a team.

A *group* is a collection of individuals. You or I could be part of a group but not have a strong sense of belonging. Even if everyone in the group is ostensibly working toward the same goal, members might not be aligned around how to achieve that goal. In short, groups don't have the strong directional relationship they need to work together effectively.

A *team* is a group that's highly aligned, meaning the members feel a sense of belonging and a shared sense of purpose. The team relationship is directional, meaning that members are guided toward something beyond just being in the relationship. This combined sense of purpose—imbued with *belonging*—is what causes a team to be effective at achieving their goals.

In other words, *groups flail while teams sail*. And belonging is the key ingredient.

THE POWER OF BELONGING

We've all been in relationship spats with other people or bumped into someone by accident, and we know there's a difference between creating friction with someone you don't know well and doing so with someone you do know well.

Let's say your neighbor's sprinkler has been spraying over the fence line and hitting your car in the driveway. If you've only exchanged a few cool "Hellos" over the past year since they moved in, you may construct a story about how they're secretly trying to get back at you for the time you blocked their parking space last week. But if you have a strong and healthy relationship with that neighbor, you're more likely to assume they didn't realize and ask them to move their sprinkler.

Your shared relationship is the foreground context for addressing friction in the relationship. Without that context, the *thing* causing the friction becomes a stand-in for the entire relationship. With context, you can say, "This *thing* isn't working, but it doesn't mean that you suck or that I don't want to be in a relationship with you." The thing that isn't working is just a small piece of the macrorelationship in which you anchor the conversation.

Belonging is what creates that shared context—that glue—in a team. It's what allows team members to give each other grace, to be patient with each other, and to offer support and solutions when they're needed. It also makes it easier for each individual team member to just show up no matter what else is going on in their lives, knowing they can be their whole selves and give their best effort without fear.

Belonging creates the cup that the energy of the team flows into and gives it shape and structure regardless of what the team does, from communication and collaboration to how a team sets goals and holds meetings. Members of high-performance teams can say, "I belong here. My team and I have a shared meaning, no matter what comes up. This is who we are and what we do."

We see this play out in high-performance teams such as military special forces, firefighters, and sports teams. The most effective ones have a high sense of belonging built into their culture. It's not just for show. It's what enables them to step up together and do what they need to do again and again.

My years of working with teams have taught me to spot quickly whether or not a team has high belonging. While low-belonging teams may be dysfunctional in a number of ways, high-belonging teams always stand out: They're more likely to meet their goals, they stay together, and they embrace hard conversations.

High-Belonging Teams Meet Goals

Readiness is your team's current capability to deliver against the requirements of its current mission. (We'll talk about readiness more in the chapter on goal-setting.)

Teams with high belonging tend to have higher readiness because where there's more belonging and trust, there tends to be more involvement in the goal-setting process. Belonging also helps with goal-setting because it gives teams space to be open and honest about where they are. Members will realize that you can still be a valuable part of the team while pointing out readiness problems without defaulting to the culture of toxic positivity, where the only option is to stay quiet or be positive.

Belonging allows team members to say, "I don't feel ready for this, I don't think that we as a team are ready for this." Belonging is the foundation for the kind of truth-telling and frank evaluation that allows you to obtain the highest levels of performance.

High-Belonging Teams Stay Together

We all want to spend our precious life hours somewhere fulfilling and be part of a team where we feel a strong sense of belonging. The more highly skilled and highly performing an individual is, the more they'll start selecting places where they truly belong and can be their best self, which is why belonging plays such a huge role in retention.

Companies lose a great deal of talent not because of pay but because of belonging. People figure out their own worth and realize that they can be great anywhere they work. Why shouldn't they work in a place that recognizes and values them for who they are?

Of course, retention—or lack thereof—has far-reaching effects and is one of the biggest predictors of high-performance teams. If a team is constantly losing team members, it gets stuck in the Tuckman cycle of forming, storming, and norming and rarely reaches the stage of performing at a high level of ease, groove, and readiness.

▢▢▢ FRAMEWORK

THE TUCKMAN TEAM DEVELOPMENT MODEL

The Tuckman Team Development Model, formulated by Bruce Tuckman in 1965, is a widely used framework that names four sequential stages of team formation: forming, storming, norming, and performing. Teams generally go through the stages in that order, with the norming stage being the one where the team establishes clear expectations and norms for how members work with each other.

There are two main factors that make the model appealing: It's easy to remember, and it helps us remember that norming comes *after* storming. The inevitability of storming isn't what's in question but the intensity of it. Many teams and novice leaders see storming as something to avoid, and by trying to bypass or thwart storming, they don't get the norming that precedes great performance.

It's also easy to forget that adding or removing a teammate creates a different team because it creates different team dynamics. Storming and norming will start again. This explains why merely adding teammates doesn't make the work go faster.

A critique of the Tuckman model—and a reason it's fallen out of favor for frameworks like the Drexler-Sibbett model—is that it doesn't provide much guidance for what to do to get your team through the stages. That's fair, and though the Drexler-Sibbett model is much more comprehensive, it's harder to remember, explain, and use in the field daily. If you'd like to learn more about how to overlay team habits with the Drexler-Sibbett model, go to teamhabitsbook.com/resources.

High-Belonging Teams Can Have Hard Conversations

Teams with high belonging communicate more clearly because they have the psychological safety, rapport, and preexisting relationships in place to ask uncomfortable questions. When we're confused about something—and we have a strong sense of belonging—we feel comfortable asking for clarification. We feel comfortable pointing out red flags and being direct when asking for what we need.

When you and I have a shared context, you can tell me I made a mistake or something isn't working without me worrying that my job is at stake. The issue at hand is just a small piece of the macrorelationship we're in rather than the whole of it.

If you're serious about changing your team's habits, you will have many hard conversations. Your entire team will need to address issues in the way you work without feeling attacked and putting up their defenses.

Belonging is created—or destroyed—by the daily habits of a team. Your team can deliberately choose to improve belonging by changing their habits or continue to let it ride at subpar levels by doing nothing.

Let's get tactical about how your team can build better habits around belonging. It all starts with walking your values.

PUT YOUR VALUES ON THE FLOOR, NOT THE WALL

A lot of organizations will post value statements on their walls, websites, or handbooks. But when you look more closely at the habits of individual teams, they're not walking the values. All those nice-sounding aspirational phrases haven't actually been integrated into the company culture.

Incorporating values into the fabric of your team culture requires a deliberate, continual effort. You need to convert those values into habits.

In the Army, the values formed the acronym LDRSHIP: loyalty, duty, respect, selfless service, honor, integrity, and personal courage. Not only were we told those values, but those values were converted into habits and behaviors that we were expected to perform. During evaluations, we were rated on how well we exhibited each of those values.

At Productive Flourishing, we do the same thing. We used to have our values listed in the "Team Core Values, Habits, and Working Guidelines" document that we send to all our teammates, but we decided that converting them into habits would make them stronger. Now, instead of listing values such as "Reliability" or "Taking Action," we list habits such as Shoot, Move, Communicate and Show Your Work (both of which are discussed in the chapter on core team habits).

It's a way of making sure our values aren't just phrases we've used as a tagline on our website. We're walking them every day.

ROCKET PRACTICE

WALK YOUR VALUES

» For each of your team or organizational values, brainstorm the behaviors you want those values to encourage. Instead of just listing your values, how can you create habits that allow your team to walk those values?

» How might you incorporate your values into performance reviews and check-ins? For example, can you tie specific actions teammates took to values and surface them in check-ins?

» Add a section to an upcoming meeting for the express purpose of having the team talk about specific habits and behaviors that manifest your team or organizational values. Suggestion: Focus first on what it means to walk a value *well* rather than on where your habits and actions are out of alignment. This focuses what might otherwise be mere critiques into practice points for excellence.

HARNESS THE STRONG POWER OF WEAK TIES

All of us—leaders, managers, and individual contributors—are people outside work. We all have full-spectrum selves that need cultivation and appreciation beyond the aspects of our personality that pertain to doing our job. Yet many organizations implicitly (or explicitly) discourage people from bringing their whole selves into the workplace.

It's almost impossible to feel a strong sense of belonging in a team where you can express only a fraction of yourself.

Why is seeing each other as whole human beings important? **Because none of us show up at the office for the sake of the job itself.** We show up for our families, pets, and passions. We show up because we love skydiving on the weekends, or because we're taking care of aging parents, or because we're supporting our spouse's fledgling business. Yes, we hope to love what we do. But we're motivated by the four-legged and two-legged beings that slip into the backgrounds of our Zoom calls or grace our desks in framed photos and by our hobbies and passions.

Every person on your team shows up with all of those things every day, even if they don't feel safe talking about them at work. When you build team habits that encourage people to bring their whole selves to work, you create space for individuals to thrive. You also make room for much deeper levels of connection among team members.

That's because belonging is built through our ties to each other, both strong and weak. Strong ties could be those things that matter a ton to you. For example, sharing an identity affinity like having the same alma mater, being from the same state, being LGBTQ+, or having the same background can be an incredibly powerful tie.

Weak ties are minor connections. Maybe my mother has the same name as yours, or we both have a dog. Maybe we share the love of a particular brand of coffee or a cult classic movie. Is that a very strong reason to bond? Probably not. But it gives us just enough to talk about at the water cooler or enough knowledge of the other person if we're going to exchange gifts around the holidays.

The more we get to know each other, the more this collection of weak ties is likely to grow, and discovering these weak ties—favorite books, songs, places to visit, or even what people put in the #random channel in Slack—enhances collaboration and communication. If you find out that a colleague shares your love of puns, you might start sprinkling them into your emails with each other as a bright spot in the day.

While a strong tie (like being the only two women in a field of mostly men) might bond you superficially, a matrix of weak ties creates a powerful chain of belonging. It not only gives you multiple points of connection but also is a good indication that you've taken the time to uncover those connections and deepen your relationship beyond one or two single obvious strong ties.

How do you build those weak ties? Start by creating a work environment where people are encouraged to share the things that are important to them outside work.

Know That the Coffee Break Isn't about Coffee

Former Starbucks president Howard Behar wrote that it's not about the coffee in his book by the same name.[1] Yet it's also *absolutely* about the coffee. When I run out to the coffee shop for an afternoon break, I don't have to ask if any of my teammates want me to pick something up. If I don't have a strong sense of belonging with my teammates, it might not occur to me. If I feel strongly connected, it might not occur to me *not* to ask.

Building belonging isn't just about ticking the box of grabbing coffee, though. *How* I ask is also important. If I offer to bring you coffee even though you've told me a dozen times you don't drink caffeine, you'll start to feel (correctly) as though I don't listen to you. If I say, "Hey, want me to grab your usual? Chamomile tea with honey, right?" it signals that I'm paying attention and care enough about you to remember what seems like a trivial detail.

On a team level, there is an explicit recognition and acknowledgment when decisions are made that factor in people's preferences. If you know one team member hates mushrooms on pizza and another is allergic to nightshades, taking that into account when you call in the pizza delivery lets them know they belong.

Of course, you don't have to call out the individual. "We're having pizza at the meeting, but because Sarah hates mushrooms, we won't have any." Instead, you can say, "We're having pizza, and we ordered a variety of styles because there are some food sensitivities and allergies. So if you don't see some of the things you like, it's just because we're trying to cater to different people with their different needs."

That may sound simple on the surface, but it shows your teammates that decisions are being made with them in mind.

Encourage People to Customize Their Environment

The COVID-19 pandemic was terrible for many people, but one of the gifts was in the massive shift to remote and virtual working in most organizations. Rather than meeting in a sterile conference room at the office, most of us were suddenly meeting via video conference from our bedrooms, kitchens, and spare rooms.

We saw each other's living environments, most of us for the first time. Kids and pets wandered into the frame. Our backgrounds displayed our hobbies and the things that were important to us: plants, *Star Wars* posters, guitars, cookbooks, family heirlooms, photographs from vacations, meaningful paintings.

This glimpse into the homes of our coworkers (combined with the general lowering of barriers in the zeitgeist because we were all exhausted and overwhelmed) helped us see each other as whole human beings in a way most of us hadn't before.

If you're working remotely, encourage people to show off places in their home that truly represent them rather than having implicit or explicit mandates that everyone set up their cameras in front of a sterile background or use filters.

In the office, you can do the same by encouraging people to decorate their desks and reconsidering clothing and attire policies. Obviously, some standards are necessary, but you can create a lot of room for people to show who they are by what they wear and what they keep on their desk.

Recognize That Chitchat Is the Main Show, Not a Distraction

Whether it's catching up about the weekend over the water cooler or posting a funny otter meme in the #random channel of your team's Slack, many organizations treat chitchat as a distraction from what team members are actually there to do.

But teams with high belonging don't just tolerate chitchat; they actively make room for it.

Build time for casual conversation into your meetings. One way is to begin the meeting by asking everyone to describe a nonwork win. Asking this simple question at the start of a weekly standup does two things.

First, it opens the door for every member of the team to share a bit about themselves outside work in a positive way. It's a way of socializing and connecting to each other human to human, which can help us extend more patience and grace to each other than when we view each other only as our roles.

Second, it primes the meeting with a positive reminder of recent wins before we get down to the sometimes thorny and frustrating business of solving problems. Starting with wins alters people's mindset about what's possible during the meeting and gives the entire team momentum and implicit bias toward being able to solve whatever's on deck this week.

This doesn't have to happen at every meeting, but asking this simple question at the start of a weekly standup is a good team habit to get into. It gets people to talk about their full-spectrum selves and the things that matter to them outside work.

One client who started this team habit found that they had two hobbyist science fiction writers on the team. These two people had been working together for nearly ten years, but neither knew they had a shared love of writing because it had never come up before. Suddenly, the two colleagues had a new tie that made their collaboration even more powerful, just because of a simple question.

At the end of the meeting, ask team members to describe their highlights from the meeting. Those highlights don't have to be from the business substance of the meeting, and in my experience of practicing this habit with my own team, they often aren't.

A highlight might be a joke or random comment that one person made. It might be learning something personal about another colleague. It might be the way that one teammate supported another who was struggling during part of the meeting.

When you really pay attention to people's highlights, you'll start to see how few of them are about the work itself and how many are about relationships. In my experience, those five or ten minutes of a meeting spent building belonging are far more valuable than the minutes you spend on a status update report that everyone could read on their own before the meeting.

Celebrate Each Other at Work

Actions go a long way, but people actually do need to *hear* how they belong and fit into the team. Celebrating wins as a group is one way to ensure that that message is spoken aloud and can provide enough fuel to drive a team through the rest of a hard week or help them have a tough conversation.

One habit to help build regular celebration into your team is to ask two questions at your monthly meetings:

1. What's a significant month-sized accomplishment that you want to celebrate?
2. What did you see another teammate do that you want to shout out?

The first question helps people practice acknowledging their own work and being seen for that work. The second question helps the team practice not only seeing other people doing great work but actively speaking to it in order to intentionally build a culture of appreciation of everyone's contributions.

Not everyone will get a shout-out in every meeting, but if you ask those two questions, by the end of the meeting, most people will feel that no matter what role they play, the team appreciates them. They'll leave the meeting excited about all the things you've accomplished and overcome together and inspired for what's next.

At Team PF, we've adopted another, more casual way of celebrating each other at work: rock-star emojis. Each member of the team chooses their own rock-star emoji, which other team members use as reactions in our messaging tool when they want to shout out that a person did a fantastic job.

ROCKET PRACTICE

INVITE OUR FULL-SPECTRUM SELVES TO WORK

» How are you signaling to your teammates that it's both acceptable and encouraged to bring your full-spectrum selves to work? In what ways can you encourage teammates to express their personality in their video call background, in the way they dress, or in how they decorate their desks?

» How does your team take note of and accommodate preferences and restrictions? For example, when scheduling meetings, are you taking religious holidays or other external schedules into account? When ordering food for the group or choosing a lunch location, are decisions being made with all teammates in mind? Might your team prefer audio-only meetings for certain kinds of conversations?

» Where can you build space into a meeting for teammates to share their wins and highlights? This could be a recurring part of the weekly standup or monthly update meeting.

» How do you celebrate wins, both at work and in team members' personal lives, as a team? How can you create a habit of acknowledging teammates who are doing amazing work and appreciating them?

BE INTENTIONAL ABOUT INCLUSION (AND EXCLUSION)

In most teams, people tend to prefer working in different ways. For example, a handful of people on the team may like to think out loud during social brainstorming sessions, but one member may think best when they can process their ideas alone or in one-on-one conversations.

Normally, one of two things happens in this scenario. Either the team member who hates social brainstorming is required to be at meetings they feel inherently awkward attending, or the team members who prefer social brainstorming sessions—with or without good intentions—start not inviting that person to the meetings.

In both scenarios, the message this sends to a team member who's more introverted or a deliberate thinker is that they don't belong on this team. Unfortunately, in many cultures, if one teammate doesn't like social brainstorming, the assumption is that something is wrong with that person. After all, it's the company culture to take part in these meetings.

A team with high belonging instead makes room for all team members to contribute how they like and do what they do best. In some cases, this looks like intentional *exclusion*. The concept of intentional exclusion is inspired by Priya Parker's book *The Art of Gathering*.[2]

Say, "I know these meetings aren't your jam. We're going to go ahead and do it, and you're welcome to join. But we set the agenda so that it doesn't include you being there and so that your feedback can be included in other ways. Feel free to attend if you want, but there's no penalty if there are other things you would rather do instead during that time."

In this scenario, the teammate doesn't feel excluded; they feel incredibly seen, understood, and appreciated.

It also improves team performance, because when you make space for everyone to contribute in the best way they can, you get the best contributions. When every teammate has chosen to be in the room, they'll give their best instead of resenting having been roped into an activity they hate.

Here are some more ways to build good team habits around inclusion.

Make Room for Deliberate Thinkers

Some people on your team will thrive on rapid-fire thinking and come to opinions and decisions quickly. Others are more deliberate processors who prefer time to mull things over and come up with a deeper, more integrated answer rather than telling you what they think off the cuff.

Make space for them by slowing down the conversation or providing ways for them to give feedback afterward. Maybe they prefer to articulate their ideas in writing. Or maybe they're happy giving their thoughts in person, but they need to be asked—and have space made to be listened to if they're not the sort of person who's comfortable wading into a heated conversation with their elbows out. Invite the quiet people and people who may not always be the top contributors to a specific meeting.

Set Inclusive Meeting Titles

The way a meeting is described can send unintentional signals about who is welcome to attend. For example, historically, only certain people at higher levels of an organization got to talk about strategy. Setting a meeting title as "Marketing Strategy Meeting" can imply that people at lower levels don't belong or have anything to contribute. Changing the title to "Marketing Planning Meeting" is a simple act that implies that everyone invited will have something to contribute. Even better would be to drop "marketing" in favor of something more specific that doesn't assume that people need specialized training to be contributing participants.

Examine your meeting titles for clarity and jargon to see who they exclude and who is invited to the table. The titles set up who really contributes, who belongs in the meeting, and who's just sitting in the meeting.

Use Descriptive Meeting Agendas

There's a bias toward leaders being extroverted, larger-than-life people who thrive on the energy created in a fast-flowing, free-form meeting. When these leaders set meetings "just to talk things out," it works for them. But for a lot of other people in the organization who might be introverts, ambiverts, or deliberate thinkers, it doesn't work to show up unprepared to a meeting or with zero context about what's needed from the conversation.

A good meeting agenda can go a long way toward creating belonging. Build the habit of sharing the meeting topic, problems to be discussed, expectations, and key outcomes in advance. This allows all team members to show up and be fully present rather than spending the first part of the meeting figuring out what's going on and how to contribute.

ROCKET PRACTICE

MAKE ROOM FOR WORK PREFERENCES

» How do you make room for teammates to contribute in the way they feel most comfortable? Remember, inclusion can sometimes mean giving a teammate the option of not showing up to a meeting. How else might they participate? For example, can they submit ideas in writing rather than attending a brainstorming session?

» When it comes to meetings, how are you soliciting contributions from your more introverted teammates or teammates who are deliberate thinkers? Are your meeting titles and agendas giving teammates the information they need to show up and be fully present?

ACKNOWLEDGE BUMPS TO MAKE THEM LESS PERSONAL

If you've ever worked in a food service environment, you know you bump into your coworkers regularly. You'll squeeze past them with a tray, or you'll elbow them as you're reaching for a bottle. It's tight quarters, people are moving fast, and if I accidentally step on your toe, I'll apologize and we'll both keep going about our work. Bumping into each other is just part of the job.

In knowledge work, we still bump into each other—though probably not physically, especially if we're working remotely. Bumps in the office happen when I send you an email but forget to include a key point, or when you forget to thread your reply to Shelly in Slack, or when Shelly saves a document in the wrong file structure.

Most of the time, these are just bumps that shouldn't be taken personally. Now, it's different if an intentional pattern of microaggression emerges that needs to be called out and dealt with in conversation. But for the most part, bumps are just part of the job.

The reason talking about bumps is useful is that it gives your team language to address these scenarios without becoming defensive. Instead of assuming intention on the part of your coworker when they forget to include the attachment and you have to ask for it—*again*—assume that you experienced a bump. With a bump, you can say, "Hey, I know you didn't mean to forget the attachment, but it's a bump we keep having. What can we set up to keep things flowing better?"

I learned this lesson in my early twenties when I was deployed overseas. I had a contentious relationship with one of my squad leaders, and one day, I got a report that this squad leader was working on something he shouldn't have been.

Because of our history of friction, my immediate response was to assume that he was going behind my back on purpose. I drove down to confront him, but before I did, I managed to take a deep breath.

Instead of asking him what the hell he thought he was doing, I calmly asked what he was working on. He explained, and it turned out that he wasn't acting maliciously at all. I was operating off a ghost plan—which we'll talk about in the chapter on planning—that hadn't been communicated to him. He was doing exactly what he should have been according to the previous version of the plan.

In business, in the military, and in life, people are moving quickly. It's easy to forget little details—just as I'd forgotten that my squad leader wasn't in the room when the plan was updated.

We never developed the best relationship, but I've always been grateful that I took a breath and approached the problem as though it were just a bump (which it was) rather than a deliberate provocation on his part. When we extend our teammates and ourselves grace and the benefit of the doubt, it allows us to address bumps without feeling defensive or attacked. It gives us the tools to communicate better and keep working together smoothly.

ROCKET PRACTICE

MANAGE BUMPS

» Where do bumps commonly occur throughout your team's process? What causes them to happen, and what can be done to address them? What team habits can be added to keep bumps from happening? What habits can be subtracted? In cases where bumps are inevitable, how can they be better communicated?

CHAPTER 3 TAKEAWAYS

- Belonging is the key ingredient for transforming a group of people into a high-performing team.
- Start walking your values by taking them off the wall and converting them into concrete team habits.
- Harness the power of weak ties by creating space for every team member to bring their full-spectrum self to work.
- Be intentional about how you include team members in (or exclude them from) projects and meetings.
- Have grace with each other when bumps occur in the workplace rather than leaping automatically to a negative assumption.

FOUR DECISION-MAKING

*The risk of a wrong decision is preferable
to the terror of indecision.*

—MAIMONIDES

When you're faced with a choice between the hummus plate or a burger and fries on your lunch break, your final decision doesn't have any effect on your team. But when you come back from lunch and choose which new product feature to develop and which to scrap, it has huge potential to affect what the rest of your team is doing.

At work, decisions are inherently social. Any choice you make affects someone else on your team or in your organization—and vice versa. Unlike your lunchtime hummus-or-burger dilemma, the path *you* decide to take on a project we're working on together immediately creates a new constraint, opportunity, or consideration for *me*.

When your team has healthy habits, decisions do what they're meant to do: keep work moving ahead while reducing the number of dropped balls and slippery handoffs (which I call Crisco watermelons) that occur along the way. But if you have poor habits, even the tiniest choices have the potential to create a quagmire.

The reason is that decisions aren't just social. They're also inherently *emotional*. Whether it's you agonizing over healthy lunch options or the team struggling to pick a new course at work, your—and your teammates'—fears, uncertainties, optimism, and other emotions are activated.

Ignoring this critical fact is why so many organizations get stuck on decision-making. They consider only the rational piece ("If I just present the right information, then everyone will come along with me") and completely miss the emotional or social component. When they face unexpected resistance from teammates who are stuck, scared, or hung up on invisible factors, they can't figure out why.

As we dive into team habits around decision-making, I want to remind you that—as with belonging in the last chapter—the way your team makes decisions will affect many other team habits. From collaboration and communication to meetings, planning, and goal-setting, improving your team decision-making habits will make positive waves through the rest of your team habits.

But first, let's take a step back to ask how decisions are made right now.

HOW DOES YOUR TEAM MAKE DECISIONS?

When young people ask me for life advice, my go-to answer is this: Your twenties aren't about *deciding* what you're going to do with your life; they're about learning how to *make decisions* so that you can decide confidently in your thirties. If you can figure out how to make decisions that are in alignment with who you are and who you want to be in the future, you'll be far better off in the following decades.

That advice tends to be deeply unsatisfying because most young people—most people in general—prefer to rush past the process of learning how to make decisions in favor of having more clarity and certainty in the moment. Most teams and organizations want to rush past that process, too. And it shows.

When teams haven't spent time learning how to make decisions, it usually manifests in three ways:

1. They assume that good decision-making will happen organically and effortlessly, which instead leads to confusion and stalling when no one takes action.
2. They swing to the opposite end of the spectrum, adopting rigid decision-making codes and frameworks that lead to wasting valuable time documenting decisions instead of actually doing the work.
3. The executives or managers have so monopolized the decision-making process that the moment they put their phone on Do Not Disturb in order to focus on their work, the work of their teams comes to a standstill.

When teams take the time to build good habits around decision-making, they see the benefits reverberate through everything else they do.

☐☐☐ FRAMEWORK

RACI

Many organizations and teams adopt frameworks to help teammates make decisions. One especially common framework that many organizations use is RACI, or who needs to be responsible, accountable, consulted, and informed.

In theory, RACI is great. It covers all the bases of making sure a decision is made and communicated to the right people. But in practice, it can bring the decision-making process to a screaming halt. Yes, we need to know who's responsible and accountable for carrying out a decision. Yes, we need to consult and inform the right people. But when we constrain decision-making to what's on a chart as opposed to what is happening in the moment, we find ourselves in a straitjacket.

It's the Law of the Instrument: When you're holding a hammer, everything looks like a nail. When you're beholden to RACI, you tend to use it to pound even the smallest decisions senseless. Nailing a RACI framework to every decision takes away from the actual act of doing the work.

When I see an organization or team clinging to a RACI process, I probe underneath to find out what they're actually trying to accomplish. Are they trying to do the work of increasing *certainty*? Or are they trying to do the work of increasing *clarity*?

If they're simply trying to increase clarity, it's usually a matter of sitting down and figuring out quickly who needs to be told and who's responsible. In a team with high belonging, this conversation can happen easily and informally without the need to create a formal RACI framework.

But a lot of the reason models like RACI exist is because people want to increase *certainty* or at least to decrease *uncertainty*.

I get the impulse. Uncertainty makes people uncomfortable. But that uncertainty and ambiguity are inherent in the shifting sands of today's workplace. The priorities your team talked about yesterday may have changed. New information might have come up or new orders been handed down. All of this creates tension between what was important yesterday (when you created the RACI), and what's emerging right now (when you're making a decision).

A RACI framework won't help you manage that tension. Instead, focus on developing your team's sense of on-the-spot clarity so they can make better decisions in the moment.

REMOVE DECISION-MAKING BOTTLENECKS

"Why isn't my team better at taking initiative?"

I hear this often from executive coaching clients, and the answer is the same nearly every time. Normally, these particular coaching clients are excellent decision-makers who built their businesses or achieved their roles within their organizations because of their ability to make decisions quickly. It's a fantastic skill, but it can have an unintended result.

Because they've placed themselves in the sole role of decision-maker, the executive or manager becomes the single point of failure

within the organization or the team. Work comes to a standstill when they're in another meeting, on vacation, or simply trying to take a few hours to clear their own plates. In these cases, a team is forced to choose between three different painful options:

1. Bug the boss and disrupt whatever else they have going on.
2. Make some decisions to keep things going and hope they don't get burned.
3. Sit on their hands until the boss is back to answer some questions and they can continue.

Teams tend to choose numbers one and three because history and organizational culture have shown that they're the safest options. Disrupting the boss sucks, but not as much as being completely stuck until the boss is back in the office. And neither of those options is as risky as choice number two. If the team rolls the dice and makes a wrong decision, it could land them in hot water.

They'd rather risk annoying the boss through interruption or inaction than risk their job by taking the initiative.

Besides the obvious drawbacks to forward momentum on projects, when an executive is the sole decision-maker, it puts a colossal amount of mental and emotional pressure on them. It feels as if they can't step out of the collaborative process even for a moment. They can't ignore that text message during their focus block because it could mean hours of lost productivity for their team. They can't set up good boundaries around communication because they need to be available at any given moment.

They can't take time to recharge their own batteries, but they also are too in demand during the workday to accomplish much meaningful work. For everyone's sake, leaders need to work with their teams to distribute the power, function, and process of making decisions.

How can you get started doing that? Start by understanding the three main types of decisions a team will have to make:

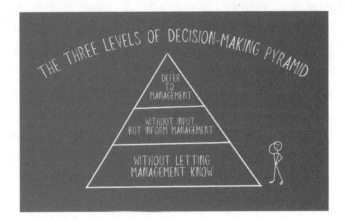

1. **Decisions that can be made without letting management know.** These are the routine decisions that teams and individual contributors make on a daily basis in order to get the job done. Should the office manager reorder printer paper when the box in the supply cabinet goes empty? Absolutely, and there's no reason for the company president to be included in the process.

2. **Decisions that can be made without input, but management needs to be informed.** Some decisions can be made by an individual contributor on their own, but management needs to know the decision was made. A good rule of thumb is that if there are obvious positive or negative fiscal, legal, or public relations repercussions, leadership should be made aware.

3. **Decisions that must be deferred to management.** These are the decisions that no one but a leader can make. Level 3 decisions are usually those that have an impact on the strategy and direction of the company.

When a team has healthy decision-making habits, level 3 decisions should take up only 5 to 10 percent of leadership's time. Unfortunately, too many decisions end up at level 3 when they shouldn't be. The goal of the team habits we will be talking about is to change that ratio, but the effect you'll be able to have will differ depending on your role.

Leaders and Managers

If you're a leader or manager who's been frustrated by your team not taking enough initiative, start by looking at how you handle these three types of decisions. On the one hand, you don't want to control the decision-making process so tightly that your team can't even order new printer paper without coming to you first. On the other hand, you don't want your team to be making senior-level decisions on their own.

The process of learning which types of decisions fall into which category is lengthy, and it's up to you as the leader to model it for your team.

Level 1 Decisions

When someone comes to you with a decision they should be capable of making on their own, encourage them to take initiative in the future by thanking them and then letting them know they can make these types of decisions without telling you in the future.

Level 2 Decisions

If you find yourself blindsided by a decision you should have been told about, clearly and calmly ask to be brought into the loop in the future. If it was a good decision, applaud the person and ask to be informed in the future. If it was a bad decision, consider this a teaching moment. Rather than chewing out your teammate (and guaranteeing that these decisions will always land on your plate in the future), teach them your decision-making process and make sure they have the information to make better decisions in the future.

Level 3 Decisions

If a teammate oversteps their bounds and makes a decision that should have been left to management, kindly let them know that in the future, all decisions of that type should be deferred to you. If it's a great decision, praise the hell out of them and consider including that person on important decision-making committees in the future.

Doing so will help democratize the decision-making process, reduce executive bottlenecks for level 1 and 2 decisions, and help clear low-level decisions off leaders' plates so they can focus on higher-level work.

Individual Contributors

As an individual contributor, it can be easy to believe that you don't have any power over how decisions are made on your team or in your organization. Maybe you've tried to change decisions you disagree with in the past and ended up in a power struggle. Whether you won or lost, you probably spent a whole lot of effort trying to make change.

When faced with decisions or a decision-making structure that you disagree with, you have two axes of approach. You can either focus your efforts on finding possibilities of doing good work with your team while accepting the constraint, or you can focus on arming yourself with the knowledge of how decisions are made within the organization in order to be in better alignment going forward.

As an individual contributor, your power question for making change is **"What's the best process for me to learn how decisions are made here?"**

Why is that question so good? First, it depersonalizes any particular decision, so you can ask it without coming across as personally attacking the decision-maker. Second, it's neutral or even positive — meaning that it's not explicitly disagreeing with a decision. It's proactive and curious.

Third, it subtly — or explicitly, depending on the culture — illuminates that there are certain reasons why decisions are being made that are not being communicated to the people they affect. A lot of intuitive leaders may not spend much time thinking about how they make decisions. When you ask a good leader this question, they might pause and try to work it through.

Asking this question can help you learn missing context around the seemingly bad decision. With that context, you may find that this was one of those tough decisions that no one liked, but it was better than the alternative choices. You might learn that there was critical information about the decision that wasn't shared with you. You might learn that the decision came from a particular point of view about strategy and purpose and mission, so while it didn't make sense on its own, it absolutely does once you have that point of view.

Whether it's a decision you liked, a neutral decision, or a decision you thought was ridiculous, the more you learn about how decisions are being made within your organization, the more you'll be able to both do your own work and advocate on behalf of your team. You're learning how to advance decisions in the organization using the actual mechanics of how decisions are being made.

Understanding how decisions are made also lays the groundwork for you to start running sprints to improve your team's decision-making habits.

 **ROCKET PRACTICE**

REMOVE DECISION-MAKING BOTTLENECKS

» If you're a leader or manager, make clear your expectations about how each decision level should be handled. Give some examples of level 1, level 2, and level 3 decisions based on team members' roles. Encourage your team to take more initiative with level 1 decisions, to communicate level 2 decisions, and to defer level 3 decisions to management.

» If you're an individual contributor, educate yourself about how decisions are made in the organization. Remember your power question for making change: "What's the best process for me to learn how decisions are made here?"

» Reference level 1, level 2, and level 3 decisions in the midst of communication and collaboration. If you're a team manager, let teammates know that a particular query or ping is a level 1 or level 2 decision. If you're an individual contributor, ask whether a particular decision is level 1 or level 2.

DEMOCRATIZE DECISION-MAKING

As the new captain of the submarine *Santa Fe*, David Marquet was stunned during a training exercise when he inadvertently gave an impossible order and his crew awkwardly attempted to carry it out rather than contradicting him. The crew had been trained to take orders rather than make decisions, even though in this instance, they had better information about the capabilities of the ship than their new captain had.

To reverse that dynamic and remove the burden of making even the smallest decisions from his own shoulders, Marquet instituted a new way of making decisions, which he details in his book *Turn the Ship Around!*[1] Rather than giving orders, he asked officers to state their intentions, starting with the phrase "I intend to." Marquet would ask clarifying questions if needed, then give his assent with "Very well."

Eventually, the leadership of the *Santa Fe* extended the idea. Ultimately, the goal became not only to state their intention but to do so in a way that outlined the plan and addressed potential objections so that Marquet didn't need to ask any more questions.

Marquet credits his "I intend to . . ." procedure with the disproportionate number of promotions that were issued to the crew and officers of the *Santa Fe*. "Eventually we turned everything upside down," he writes. "Instead of one captain giving orders to 134 men, we would have 135 independent, energetic, emotionally committed and engaged men thinking about what we needed to do and ways to do it right. This process turned them into active leaders as opposed to passive followers."

Intent-based decision-making puts the onus of going through the pros and cons of the decision on the shoulders of the person who's doing the work rather than their supervisor. It also trains them to think like a manager because in order to state their intention and receive a "Very well" in response, they need to have thought through potential objections and explain how their decision addresses them. As we discussed above, they need to understand how decisions are made within the organization.

Intent-based decision-making also addresses two common problems with the way many organizations make decisions: Either they're made by people who aren't close to the work (such as Marquet issuing a detailed order about a set of controls he was unfamiliar with), or people shift responsibility for actually making decisions back onto their boss's plate.

Who's Closest to the Work?

Executives and leaders are, by the very nature of their jobs, removed from the day-to-day tasks performed by less senior members of their teams. The CEO is unlikely to be answering the customer service line, overseeing account activations, or filing burrs off widgets on the production floor. Yet in too many companies, critical decisions that affect those customer service team members, account representatives, and production-line workers are made without consulting them.

Even when the distance between the roles isn't so vast, many organizations still have team decision-making habits where, when a decision needs to be made, a team member needs to stop their work, go to the manager, explain the situation, and then receive a decision that they take back to their teammates.

Worse than the work stoppage while a decision is acquired is the fact that this creates a constant lag time while decisions are relayed. A liaison may come back from the leader to say, "We need to do X, Y, and Z." By the time the team starts doing X, Y, and Z, the leader may have different information or have updated their decision.

Intent-based decision-making moves the decision closer to the point of the work it impacts by putting the responsibility for gathering all the pertinent facts on the person most likely to be affected by the decision itself. Even if the final "Very well," "Hold off," or "Let's try this instead" still comes down to the manager or leader, they're making decisions with a much clearer view of the problem than before.

Who Owns the Question?

One of my coaching clients was working through a massive paradigm shift for his organization. It had started out as a very top-down model, where the founder (my client) made decisions and passed them down to the team to implement. The team might give information back to the founder in order to inform his decisions, but ultimately, the founder was the sole decision-maker.

Like David Marquet, my client wanted to shift his organization to a model where his entire organization was empowered to make decisions rather than piling them all on his plate. One way we did this was by changing the way his team approached the decision-maker role. Instead of asking, "Who owns this decision?" his organization started to ask, "Who owns this question?"

The reason this is important is because when you own a question, it's not solely your responsibility to come up with an answer. You have to obtain it through consensus. But, as the owner, it *is* your responsibility to keep asking that question until it is solved and do whatever you can to help the team come to a consensus-based decision around the question.

With this model, you still have responsibility, which is important. But you don't end up with unilateral power, where one person makes a decision and others don't have a chance to weigh in.

Who's Got the Monkey?

I regularly send executive coaching clients a 1974 management classic from the *Harvard Business Review* titled "Who's Got the Monkey?"[2] Some of the language is dated by today's standards, but the problem discussed by the authors, William Oncken, Jr., and Donald L. Wass, is more relevant than ever. The "monkey" from the article is the work that is a subordinate's responsibility until it jumps from the subordinate to the boss.

Upward delegation—when a problem that should be handled by an individual contributor ends up being handed back up to their manager—has always been a problem in the workplace. These days, as our organizations have become flatter, we tend not to be explicit about who delegates, who is delegated to, and the consequences of not doing what's been delegated. Because of this, the delegator is often seen more as a coworker who can share a monkey than as the person who gives and blocks monkeys.

What happens is that a manager or leader is doing their own work when a teammate comes to them with a problem. The manager says, "Sure, I can help you with that," and takes the problem onto their own plate. The team-mate tackles a different task from their list and then clocks out at the end of the day feeling that their job is done. Meanwhile, the manager is still at work dealing with all the monkeys that hopped onto their desk.

Building a team habit of intent-based communication helps keep monkeys on the right desks because it requires the decision-maker to un-pack why they're making a decision and outline what they've considered rather than delegating the decision back up to leadership.

This can particularly be a help with level 2 decisions because a team member will often propose a decision while actually putting the burden of thinking through all the considerations back on their manager. When the goal is to provide leaders with enough context that they can quickly say "Go ahead" or "Hold off" without having to ask for more clarification, the burden of making the decision is shifted back to the teammate and helps them develop that skill so that over time, they can make the deci-sion and notify leadership rather than seeking approval.

Intent-based decision-making is also excellent for lateral communica-tion between teammates. Instead of saying, "Hey, I'm thinking of doing X; what do you think?" they can say, "I'm thinking of doing X. Here's what I've considered to make that decision. Can you see anything that I'm missing?" This not only keeps work running more smoothly but also lowers the emotional, social, and mental load of the team.

One useful shortcode (we'll discuss shortcodes more thoroughly in the chapter on communication) for assisting intent-based decision-making is the acronym DRIP: decision, recommendation, intention, or plan. "Here's the problem as I understand it. My DRIP is to solve it by doing X."

At its root, the idea of "Who's got the monkey?" is about who owns the responsibility to see something through. It invites us to be on the lookout for the ways we give our monkeys to others as well as the ways others try to pass monkeys on to us.

When your team is more rigorous about defining who, in fact, has the monkey, it introduces much more clarity regarding who's respon-sible for making and carrying out certain decisions. It also introduces language to describe and deal with the discomfort when monkeys that should be part of one person's job or responsibilities are continually handed off to someone else because of the first person's struggles to manage their monkeys.

This is particularly true for many female leaders and leaders of color who need to find an authentic, powerful way of saying, "That's not my problem." Many women and people of color have not been socialized to push back when others implicitly or explicitly ask them to take on additional work. When you normalize this way of pointing out which role should have responsibility, it creates space for everyone to do their best work without being overwhelmed by other people's monkeys.

This isn't something that just management can solve. Regardless of what the boss is doing, individual contributors and their teammates can partner up to identify when monkeys are being passed among team members and come up with solutions.

Why "Somebody" Never Does Anything

Most teams tend to have the same silent team member who's constantly dropping the ball. A slacker named "somebody."

Somebody was supposed to call the vendor to renegotiate the contract. Somebody was supposed to make sure the office supply closet is always stocked with printer ink. Somebody was supposed to tell Lauren that the meeting time was changed from 1 p.m. to 3 p.m.

But **"somebody" never does anything**—even though many teams keep them on the payroll.

When teams have a poor decision-making flow, it's often a problem of an unclear responsibility flow. Even if a decision was reached during a meeting, if no one is given responsibility to execute it after the meeting, it doesn't get done. The team as a group is expecting somebody to step up and handle it, but a decision about whose responsibility it is was never made.

Sometimes, a team thinks they *have* assigned responsibility. Shana and Masud are supposed to work on it, after all. The problem is that when two people are responsible for a task, it's very likely to fall into the gap between those two people. One person will assume that the other has taken responsibility for it, and vice versa.

This is obviously frustrating, but there is a simple solution. Even if multiple people have responsibility for accomplishing a certain task or making a decision, when it comes time for direction, one person needs to be responsible for making sure it gets done.

(We'll talk more about how to do this in the chapter on collaboration.)

 **ROCKET PRACTICE**

DEMOCRATIZE DECISION-MAKING

» How removed are decisions from the people actually doing the work in the organization? What can you do to move the decisions closer by using Marquet's "I intend to . . ." procedure for level 1 and level 2 decisions and by soliciting more input for level 3 decisions?

» Rather than giving one person responsibility for making a decision, create a team habit of asking who owns the question. As the question owner, who else needs to be involved to make the decision? What will it take to reach a consensus?

» Does your team have a habit of giving each other monkeys? Practice normalizing pushing back in a way that empowers the asker to own the question and come up with a solution rather than passing the problem on.

» Is it clear who is responsible for carrying out a decision once it has been made? Or are you relying on "somebody" to step up?

MAKING BETTER DECISIONS AS A TEAM

Decision-making can be hard enough when we're choosing between options on our own. When the group gets involved, it becomes even more complicated. Good team decision-making habits are about lessening the cognitive, emotional, and social load of the people around you in order to

push the work forward, but many teams haven't spent much time thinking about how to share that power. **When you improve your team habits
around decision-making, you enable true team partnership, collaboration, and sanity for individuals on the team.**

Keep a Decision Log

One of the reasons we end up with broken printers is that no one knows
what decisions and assumptions led to their existence, so no one knows
how to fix them. Keeping a decision log helps people understand how
decisions are being made because it documents not only the *what* of the
decision but also the *why*.

It doesn't take long to write an entry in a decision log, whether you
use a tool like Notion, Confluence, or any internal record-keeping solution. But it makes a huge difference in people's ability to understand
what's going on in terms of decisions.

First, our memories are just not as good as we think they are. Two
years down the road—even two days if things are hectic—the reasons behind why we made certain decisions can become murky. All that debate,
research, and fact-gathering that you did in the moment have vanished
into the recesses of your mind. And if you weren't present at the moment
of the decision? You'll have no clue.

The second reason to publish your decisions is that it shifts the conversation from just a quick yes or no to a great tool for teaching people how decisions are made. It shows that most important decisions are
made by weighing different assumptions and different constraints and
gives everyone insight into the broader system in which these decisions
are being made.

Third, it forces you to articulate your assumptions, which helps you
make stronger decisions.

Every decision has baked-in assumptions behind it, whether they're
explicitly acknowledged or implicit biases. As I write this, my team is in
the middle of deciding whether our new Momentum app will inherit
our Productive Flourishing Instagram account or whether we'll start a

new one specifically for it. There are compelling arguments in both the pro and con columns, and we're making certain assumptions whichever direction we go.

In this case, the obvious assumption is that Instagram will be an effective channel to promote Momentum. By writing up the decision, we're articulating that assumption and opening it up to discussion from the rest of the team. We're also doing our future selves a favor because whichever decision we make, when we look back in a few years to evaluate whether it was a success, we can also assess our underlying assumptions.

Build Time into Complex Decisions

The thing about assumptions, though, is that it can take time to bring them to the surface. If your organization is constantly springing decisions on the team without giving them a heads-up, you're missing a major opportunity to gather input and make stronger decisions.

At Productive Flourishing, we've learned that we need a two-week cycle to properly work through most major decisions. Two weeks before we want to make a final decision, one team member (usually me in the case of decisions that affect the entire company) will propose a course of action and tentative plan.

The following week, we'll gather the team again to ask for additional thoughts about the decision. This gives everyone a chance to sleep on the idea or break into smaller groups to have different conversations about the decision. Team members might spend some time researching. This gives the idea some time to aerate and gives team members a chance to interrogate their initial emotional reactions. It also allows time for questions and concerns to surface.

In the second meeting, we reiterate the tentative decision and ask the team, "Now that you've had some time to think about it, how does it land with you? Do you have any concerns? Any questions? Did any issues come up over the past week?"

Giving team members time to sit with a major decision prevents you from making hasty, ill-formed decisions because it builds opportunities to strengthen the plan in the decision-making schedule. It also incorporates all the different ways in which people process information, which we talked about in more depth in the chapter on belonging.

Think of aerating decisions like aerating wine. It allows you to see the full dimensions of the decision and creates a smoother and more satisfying process.

Leave the Van down by the River

We have a very human tendency to consider decisions high stakes and irreversible even though most actually are not. We can fall into three traps:

1. This decision has extremely high stakes: Deciding one way or the other could have catastrophic outcomes.
2. This decision can't be reversed: If I make this one decision, then that's the way it will be for the rest of my work life.
3. This decision can't be recovered from: If the outcome is catastrophic, we'll never be able to claw our way back.

Most of our decisions—individual or team—are not that way. But because of the social and emotional components involved in team decisions, we tend to apply higher stakes to them.

To be fair, even relatively insignificant team decisions do have higher social stakes than ones we make on our own. When you choose a new pho restaurant for Friday's team lunch, you feel a personal responsibility for picking a good restaurant. If the food sucks, your head trash might start telling you a story: You lost status. Your team will never trust you to choose a restaurant again—and in fact, they probably have lost trust in you overall. That means that pretty soon, you'll be at the bottom of the team, they'll be looking for a way to fire you, and you'll find yourself living in a van down by the river, as Matt Foley, Chris Farley's famous motivational speaker character on *Saturday Night Live*, would say.

This tendency to spiral toward the worst-case scenario—the Van down by the River fallacy—is a frequent problem for individuals but also affects the team's decision-making mentality. As a team, we agonize over the potential negative ramifications of the decision, allowing our imagination to paint doom-filled pictures that keep us from charging forward.

Sure, if you're in a military scenario, one bad decision can cost lives or create years of international turmoil. But most of us aren't in that situation. Most of us aren't astronauts or doctors. Most of our decisions, especially if our team has an agile experimentation mindset, are low stakes, reversible, and recoverable.

 **ROCKET PRACTICE**

MAKE SMARTER TEAM DECISIONS

» Start keeping a decision log. Where will you record decisions that are made and the assumptions that supported them?

» Where can you build additional time into the process of making complex decisions? At what points can you solicit feedback from the team along the way in order to allow questions to surface, address concerns, and strengthen the decision? What's the right amount of aeration time for your team that keeps it moving along but doesn't rush the decision?

» When you notice your team playing out the Van down by the River fallacy, name it, claim it, and tame it. Say, "Hey, we're doing that Van down by the River thing again. What can we do to make this decision lower stakes, reversible, and recoverable so we can actually try it out?" Then try the thing. If it doesn't work out, move on.

» If your team is stuck on a decision, sometimes the best way to get them unstuck is not to address the rational reasons but rather to ask, "What do we feel about this decision? Why is this such a gripping thing that's got us torn? What are the social consequences of this decision that might be making it more difficult?" Asking these questions can help the team get moving again.

ARE MAYBE DECISIONS PROBLEMATIC? MAYBE

In an ideal world, when you sit down to make a decision with your teammates, you end up with a clear "Yes" or "No." But a lot of times, the answer actually turns out to be "Maybe." Is that a big problem? Not necessarily, depending on what's going on. Usually, one of three things is happening when a decision ends in maybe.

It's Not Clear How a Decision Might Be Made

In this case, the question being asked is actually more of an idea or suggestion with no clear anchor points for how to make the decision. The best course of action here is to chart out the information requirements that would help move the issue from an open question to a solid decision.

Ask, "What would need to be true of the world or our team for this to be a clear yes or no?" In other words, what additional information do you need?

It's Not Clear Who Owns the Decision

Everyone in the room might think the question is interesting or even a great idea. The only problem is that no one in the room knows whether they can make a decision about that idea. Or, conversely, everyone might think it's a terrible idea but not know if they have the autonomy to do anything about it.

The question to ask is "Who else needs to be in this conversation in order to achieve a clear yes or no?"

It's Not Clear Where this Decision Fits into the Priority Stack

Remember, every important decision affects downstream work or current work. Sometimes, we may have all the information we need and the right people in the room, but we're still unclear about how the decision itself will affect other priorities. Because of this, we can't firmly say yes or no.

The way to address this problem is to obtain clarity on how a yes or no decision will affect downstream decisions. In this instance, engaging in some microscenario planning can go a long way toward helping you achieve clarity.

Start by pretending the answer to the decision is yes, and play out how that would look. What else does it affect? What priorities does it address? Who would need to be told about it? What are the potential ramifications? Go through the same exercise as though the answer to the decision is no.

When you're dealing with a maybe decision, you first need to answer whether that decision is important enough to push it to a yes or no. If yes, who's responsible for ensuring that we get to an answer, and what's the process for doing that? If no, how do we codify or communicate that this remains a maybe so that the next time it pops up, we know it's an open question and won't reopen the project again?

At Productive Flourishing, we do this by including a section in our team documents called Open Questions. When a member of Team PF notes something there, it indicates that we don't know the answer to that question yet, but we're going to ask it. This keeps other team members from becoming stuck on these known unknowns.

The question then becomes, is that known unknown important enough to solve? Or is there positive value in leaving it as a maybe for now?

⬜⬜⬜ FRAMEWORK

KNOWN KNOWNS, KNOWN UNKNOWNS, AND UNKNOWN UNKNOWNS

The phrase "known unknowns" may sound odd, but it comes from former US secretary of defense Donald Rumsfeld. He said that there are known knowns (things we know we know), known unknowns (things we're aware we do not know), and unknown unknowns (things we don't know we don't know).

Politics aside, it's a useful framework for thinking about the realm of information and data that inform your decisions.

We don't necessarily need to solve for the known knowns, and the unknown unknowns are so impossible to plan for that they're not worth worrying too much in a business context. Unknown unknowns are one of the reasons you bring in outside consultants who can help you plan for those.

Once you name an unknown unknown, however, it becomes a known unknown. For example, "What will this VUCA environment throw our way next?" is an unknown unknown. "Will we see another pandemic disrupt business as we know it in the next decade?" or "Is a recession on the horizon?" are known unknowns—which can be quite valuable to explore.

This framework is helpful when making a decision, for example, if you're interviewing a new candidate for a job, consider the following:

» Known knowns: We know what's on their résumé, how the team feels about them, how well they answered interview questions, etc.

» Known unknowns: We don't know how much their résumé actually indicates what they can do or how stable this role will be over the next three to six months.

» Unknown unknowns: We have no idea what might pop up to complicate this hire that we haven't yet discovered.

Sometimes, leaving an open question open helps the team think about their habits in a way that leads to important insights down the road. This is especially the case for startups and scale-ups going through a transition or wanting to keep their opportunities open. Other organizations experiencing a VUCA environment can also benefit by leaving a maybe open intentionally as a reminder that sometimes you need to question certain assumptions or look at a problem from a different direction.

Leaving an intentional maybe can open up new insights, leading to the next big-I or little-i innovation in your team.

ROCKET PRACTICE

ADDRESS MAYBES

» When the answer to a decision is "Maybe," determine the cause. Do you need additional information to make the decision? Is it unclear who has the authority to make the decision? Is this not currently a priority, and do you need to table the decision for later?

» Add a section to project documents for "known unknowns," and include who is responsible for finding further information. For example, "Cost is unknown. Jaime has reached out to the vendor for a quote and will update when he hears back."

CHAPTER 4 TAKEAWAYS

- Decisions aren't just social. They're also inherently *emotional*. Ignoring the emotional or social component in favor of the purely rational piece is where many organizations get stuck.
- Remove decision-making bottlenecks by understanding the three levels of decisions a team needs to make and acting accordingly:
  - Decisions that can be made without letting management know.
  - Decisions that can be made without input, but management needs to be informed.
  - Decisions that must be deferred to management.
- Use intent-based decision-making to empower teammates at all levels to own decision-making for their own roles.
- Understand that most decisions are not as high stakes and irreversible as we think they are.

FIVE GOAL-SETTING AND PRIORITIZATION

The worst walls are never the ones you find in your way.
The worst walls are the ones you put there.

—URSULA K. LE GUIN

Everybody wants to be on the winning team.

You know the feeling: Your team is lining up goals and knocking them out of the ballpark again and again. Even better, those goals are in the Goldilocks zone of challenging but not impossible, you and your teammates have meaningful reasons to care about hitting your targets, and you're aligned around what work is top priority. Best of all, you leave work each day knowing you moved the needle because your efforts are aligned around projects that are closely tied to the company's overall strategy.

Unfortunately, most of us have also had the exact opposite experience. Our day-to-day work isn't tied into anything we personally care about, which makes it start to feel meaningless. Team efforts are misaligned because no one can agree on priorities, which causes friction and inertia as team members work at odds with each other. And even when the team does push a goal across the finish line, it doesn't feel like a victory because it's inconsequential to the overall business plan.

The difference between these two scenarios has less to do with how objectively amazing the team is than with their goal-setting and prioritization habits. That's good news because improving those habits is something you have control over. Whether you're the executive defining strategy, the manager translating strategy into goals, or the individual contributor trying to find more meaning and alignment in your daily work, building better team habits around goal-setting and prioritization can make a massive difference in your team's ability to win.

Good goal-setting and prioritization team habits help people understand not just what needs to be done right now but also how their work supports the overall goals of the team and how those goals are ultimately informed by company strategy.

In this chapter, we will discuss the psychology of choosing which goals to advance as well as team habits that help us prioritize those goals. But first we need to ask a question that often gets breezed past when goals are being set in the first place.

HOW READY IS YOUR TEAM?

Readiness is a topic that military personnel, firefighters, sports teams, and people in operations think about a great deal, but it's not something that many people on business teams pay attention to. However, if you're not thinking about readiness, how can you expect your team to have high performance?

Readiness is exactly what it sounds like: the capability of a team or individual to accomplish their goals, complete their projects, and perform to standard. A team with low belonging and poor team habits will have a lower level of readiness than one with extremely high belonging and performance. The problem is that many goals are set without taking readiness into account. This sets the team up to fail in one of two ways: 1) They will not achieve the goal, or 2) they will succeed, but only at such extraordinary effort and expense—Dunkirk spirit—that the bill will come due. They'll be worn out or burned out, or they'll spend far more resources than you expected to get it done.

☐☐☐ FRAMEWORK

DUNKIRK SPIRIT

Dunkirk spirit is the pattern in which, despite terrible planning and decision-making, a team rallies and accomplishes a daunting goal through valiant efforts, long hours, and sheer tenacity. "Dunkirk" refers to the courageous efforts of the English civilian sailors who rescued the British Expeditionary Force (BEF) during the Battle of Dunkirk in World War II. I originally wrote about this before the movie *Dunkirk* told the tale.

One of the worst aspects of a team channeling Dunkirk spirit is that it can set the bar for the effort and performance expected of a team. Not only does this lead to a team culture of burnout, it also removes the focus from the conditions that led to Dunkirk spirit being needed in the first place. Because the team can rise at the last minute and get it done, the team habits that prevent the need for last-minute Dunkirk spirit are not cultivated.

When you see Dunkirk spirit, know what it truly is: poor planning, faulty decision-making, and unrealistic expectations. Acknowledge and appreciate the hard work the team put in to save the day, but don't put them in the position where expecting heroic efforts is the norm. Save heroic efforts for the unforeseeable, unpredictable scenarios that we all understand happen every so often.

Either way, the team fails, but it was never the team's fault—it was the fault of whoever set the goals. If you don't have an honest idea of your team's readiness level, you can't set reasonable goals.

Unfortunately, what usually happens is that people think about readiness *after* a major project or event has happened when they're investigating why the team didn't meet expectations. In the after-action review or postmortem—assuming there is one—leaders are often surprised at how underprepared the team was to meet their expectations.

You know who usually isn't surprised? The team. **Most teams know exactly how ready they are, even if they don't have the space or language to express it.**

A simple starting point when thinking about readiness is to look at your team's competency (Do we know how to do it?) and capacity (Do we have the bandwidth to do it?). That's not the whole story, though. Many teams with the know-how and bandwidth still aren't able to get the job done. They also need the team habits that allow them to apply know-how and bandwidth *together*.

Focusing on improving a team's habits is also one of the fastest ways to get to a higher readiness level; improving capacity and competency takes longer. For capacity, you either need to pull people off projects or hire new people. For competency, you need time and practice. Improving your team habits can immediately free up capacity by removing the broken printers and preempting the Crisco watermelons that make work harder than it needs to be. It also increases competency by creating winnable learning opportunities for people to practice their skills.

The rest of this chapter will help you build team habits that will steadily improve your team's goal-setting and prioritization habits, but a major facet of readiness is also belonging, which we talked about in Chapter 3. Teams with a stronger sense of belonging are more tightly knit and better prepared. They also feel more comfortable speaking up to say, "Hey, I don't feel like we as a team are ready for this," which allows for better goal-setting.

How ready is your team? You'll find more information and a readiness assessment at teamhabitsbook.com/resources.

☐☐☐ FRAMEWORK

CONE OF UNCERTAINTY + TUCKMAN'S STAGES OF GROUP DEVELOPMENT

Layering two frameworks can help explain how good goal-setting team habits impact a team's performance over time.

Cone of Uncertainty: The number of unknowns in a project typically decreases over time, which means that the margin of error in decision-making, goal-setting, and prioritization becomes smaller the closer you come to the end of the project. The more you learn about the project, the more you understand it, and the more realistic your goals will be.

Tuckman's Stages of Group Development: Teams go through four stages of development in their life cycle: forming, storming, norming, and performing (see the sidebar in Chapter 3).

When you lay the Tuckman model over the Cone of Uncertainty, you can see why teams perform better the longer they stick with a project. They develop a much stronger foundation of knowledge, context, default agreements, and expectations over time, which allows them to set (and achieve) smarter goals.

This is a helpful concept for individual contributors, managers, and executives to understand why so many errors, missteps, and fumbles happen—especially in the earliest parts of a project, when things are more uncertain. Things will become better if you stick with it. However, every time you change teams, change the plan, change the goal, or change the expectations, you start a new Cone of Uncertainty.

Changing goals and expectations midstream is extremely disruptive, whether you're a leader setting annual goals, a manager setting monthly goals, or an individual contributor setting weekly or daily goals. Layering these framework models shows why the general best practice is to stick with the objective and key results you started with for the entire cycle, even—and especially—if you're wrong. It's better to see a wrong goal through for a quarter and learn from it than to change your targets or goals midway. It's counterintuitive but effective.

CHOOSE PULL GOALS OVER PUSH GOALS

Most of us have too much on our plates, which means that every day, we're faced with the question of what to prioritize, what to back-burner, and what to simply not do. If we were perfectly rational creatures who made perfectly rational choices, we would choose the goals that have the most strategic impact or that make the most rational sense.

It turns out that we're actually organic beings who choose goals and tasks based on a number of nonrational factors. Our decision-making process includes external factors like how we'll be rewarded or punished as well as emotional elements like what's easiest or most fun. But we also decide based on factors such as what will be most rewarding because of the challenge involved or because it's closely tied to our purpose and passion.

Yes, we're all here to do a job. The desire to stay employed and get that paycheck is absolutely a good motivator. But work doesn't need to be a four-letter word. It can be joyful, meaningful, and enriching when we understand the emotional components around how goals are moved forward. The more we try to discount our irrational human nature, the more difficult it is for our teams to align on and advance goals.

Avoiding Sticks or Chasing Carrots

Pain can be a powerful motivator, but it's hard to motivate people by pain and fear for the long haul. Turns out pain doesn't create the best creative work environment or the best morale. It doesn't create great belonging, and as we've already discussed, a strong sense of belonging is key to good team habits across all the other categories.

Reward can also be a powerful motivator, and most of us agree that the carrot is better than the stick. But carrots tend to create many perverse incentives because people will alter their team habits and scenarios in order to win—sometimes maliciously, sometimes not—the game that's put in front of them.

As a side note, the twisted relationship with reward motivators is one of the challenges of startups, where a reward culture is often built around people achieving goals that the company sometimes doesn't last long enough to make good on. That fear of failure and hope for rewards that may or may not come wash people out.

In *Drive: The Surprising Truth about What Motivates Us*, Daniel Pink digs deeper into the problems with extrinsic motivations like sticks and carrots.[1] Complex, conceptual, or creative tasks in particular can suffer when the motivation is purely to avoid pain or earn a reward.

Taking the Easy Road or Finding a Challenge

Another common human tendency is to choose to prioritize what's easy. We just want to get through the day and go home. Finding that shortcut and place of ease is the most rational or sensible thing to do—in the face of a busy day, we have to choose our wins, after all.

We're wired to make life easier for ourselves. *And*, counterintuitively, we might also find goals that are challenging more appealing. In a competition between an easy goal and an ambitious goal, a team with high belonging and performance might have a bias toward the ambitious one. Those teams know the reward of meeting a challenge and know that it's worth the risk of falling short.

This is often the case in organizations where innovation is rewarded and cultivated. In organizations and teams where winning and completing are rewarded over choosing more daring goals, teams tend to default to the easier goal.

Another example is when we're pursuing mastery of a subject; even when we get to the part of the work that isn't as easy or fun as the project was at first, the reward of mastery is a powerful motivator. Daniel Pink lists it in his book *Drive* as a key factor in intrinsic motivation, along with autonomy and purpose.

Playing the Boss's Game or Making Up Our Own

Another no-brainer choice that we tend to make is fun over not fun. When all other factors are the same, we'll often choose a goal that seems fun as opposed to one that sounds boring.

This is where gamification comes in handy as a motivator. We humans are remarkably good at defining a game, even if it's something as simple as spotting license plates from other states when we're on a road trip. There's no point system or external reward, but we still get a burst of dopamine from every new license plate we find once we've decided to play the game.

At work, we use tokens, achievement icons, certifications, badges, and internal competitions to gamify our jobs. However, we don't always take into account whether the game we're incentivizing teams to play is aligned with business goals or whether it's a game they want to play. For example, if you're running a design competition and the team really wants to win, they'll make it a priority. If they were signed up without being consulted, it'll be just one more thing on their plates. And if it's actively a distraction from more important goals, then you've shot yourself in the foot by incentivizing them to play instead of staying focused on other work.

Doing Work That Matters to Ourselves and the Team

Maslow's hierarchy of needs would predict that, given the choice between mere survival and self-actualization, people will gravitate toward survival. This concept has a hard time explaining obvious choices of self-actualization that put our survival at risk, such as joining the military or becoming a firefighter. It also doesn't explain why people will choose to work themselves into a state of burnout and sickness in order to be good team players. Yet the reality is that people choose to do things that put their physical well-being in jeopardy for reasons of self-actualization, purpose, and belonging all the time.

We want to do work that matters. We want to know that every widget we forge, spreadsheet we fill out, or customer complaint we answer is making a difference. If we know it is, we're more likely to want to step up to that goal. If not, we'll find something that's more fun, is easier, or is otherwise incentivized.

This could mean doing work that aligns with your own values or the organization's values or that makes life better for your team in general. (As a side note, this is the motivation most likely to pull you through doing the work around changing team habits.)

Every team and every individual has a different inherent set of motivations when it comes to choosing which goals to advance. When you understand that, it allows you to tap into the powerful team habit of creating pull goals.

Pull Goals versus Push Goals

Knowing how people choose can help you come up with goals that are extrinsically more motivating than others. But not every business goal can be rewarded, easy, and fun. That's why it's important to understand what—specifically—intrinsically motivates you and your team and to create goals that activate those factors.

Push Goals Require More Motivational Effort to Keep People Going

If you find yourself coming back to remind people about what you're doing and why, it's probably a push goal. The team isn't inherently motivated to do the thing on their own. They're often doing the minimum required to get it done because they either don't understand why it's important or they're trying to tick a box in order to get back to what they really want to be doing.

Pull Goals Require Less Management Because People Are More Inherently Inclined to Do Them

When the road gets rocky, people persevere because there's a sense of meaning and purpose behind what they're working on. Pull goals also tend to create more collaboration and cooperation among the group.

It's the difference between filling out the dreaded weekly report, which you always need to remind your team to send in by Friday, versus the challenge or problem that the team shows up ready to crack each morning.

It usually doesn't take much effort to convert a push goal into a pull goal. Here are some examples of this conversion.

Take revenue goals, for example. Senior leaders want to see more revenue growth, so they often impose revenue goals on teams, but making more money for the company isn't an inherently motivating goal for most people.

What *can* be inherently motivating is converting that revenue goal into the number of people served or helped. If I worked at Disney World, I wouldn't care about the dollar amount of ticket sales. I would instead think about that iconic summer experience that a family is having. The family standing in line saved money for the cost of the tickets, the hotel room, and the flights—all so their kids could have a once-in-a-childhood experience. As a Disney employee, I might not be motivated by the dollar amount represented by how many families I sold tickets to each day. But I could absolutely care about giving each family an amazing experience.

As another example, maybe my job is cranking out safety widgets. The number of units probably isn't inherently motivating on its own, but when I reframe it to think that each unit I crank out represents a potential life saved, that's a powerful motivator.

Whatever your job within the organization, your work affects those around you. Maybe you don't care one bit about the abstract value of the number that ends up in cell C17 of the spreadsheet you fill out each week, but you absolutely care about the fact that cell C17 represents your team getting a bonus. Even if you're in a position where the bonus isn't a big deal, it could mean a lot to your teammate who just had a kid or who's caring for a parent or who's saving for that trip to Disney World that they never got to go on as a child.

ROCKET PRACTICE

CONVERT PUSH GOALS TO PULL GOALS

» If you're a senior leader, understand the intrinsic motivations of your teams and create goals that are aligned with those motivators. This requires you to get to know your teams well enough to understand what motivates them as well as ensuring that each strategic initiative and subgoal is aligned with your company values.

» If you're a middle manager, you're probably trapped between the senior leaders who want to accomplish some big strategic initiative and your team, who are buried by other work. Your job is to do the up-and-down translation so that everybody's on the same page. If your team has pull goals they're excited about, you may need to translate those goals into things that matter to senior leaders. If it's the inverse, where the senior leaders have a big strategic business goal that doesn't resonate with your team, you may need to convert it into a game that inspires your team.

» If you're an individual contributor and you have some empathy for your team leaders or managers, you probably realize that senior leaders and managers often just don't have time—or know enough about what drives you—to create good pull goals for you. That doesn't mean you can't convert a push goal to your own pull factors. You don't have to wait for your senior leaders and managers; you can inject a bit more meaning, purpose, and value into a mundane business goal in order to get yourself—and your teammates—more excited about it.

TURN GOALS INTO PRIORITIES: THE TEAM COST OF EVERY GOAL

It doesn't matter how strong a pull factor a goal has if it's not actually assigned the resources to make it a priority. Every project costs four things:

time, energy, attention, and money (TEAM). If accomplishing a certain goal really is a priority, then that will be reflected in team and individual schedules (time) and focus (energy and attention) as well as in the budget (money).

Time: Our Schedules Define Our Priorities

When I first started coaching executives and teams about advancing goals within their organizations, I started by looking at the people who made up their teams. These days, I start by looking at those people's calendars.

Mahatma Gandhi said, "It's not just words. Action expresses priorities." At work, the schedule is what drives our actions every day. People's schedules are their priorities, like it or leave it, and **if you really want your team to advance a goal, it needs to take up space on their calendar.**

What's on your schedule determines what you'll be able to push forward, but many people do not have 100 percent free choice about what's on that schedule.

Why does this matter? Many leaders look at achieving a goal as an individual's choice: They either decided to focus on that, or they didn't. But the less schedule autonomy someone has, the less goal autonomy they have. Is the way a person's schedule is set up conducive for them to be able to choose the goals that matter most? Or are we expecting them to tackle really big problems with the dregs of time left over between the meetings that turned their schedules into unmanageable Swiss cheese?

Unfortunately, no matter where you are in the hierarchy, you're probably forced to push really big goals forward in the dregs of your time or take work home in order to concentrate on it in the evenings and weekends, when you have schedule autonomy. While that may seem like a great deal from an employer's perspective, it's not a great deal from the perspective of the employee, their family, or their community.

Incidentally, giving someone more control over their schedule isn't just important for their ability to pursue organizational and team goals. It's also one of the best indirect ways to build belonging and improve happiness and morale.

No-Meeting Days

One way to give the entire team the time they need to focus on priorities is by carving out swaths of time in the entire team's schedules that are designated as meeting-free.

At Productive Flourishing, we have No-Meeting Thursdays, where a meeting specifically means more than two people having a scheduled conversation. Now, if I'm working on something and you're working on the same thing, and we need to have a fifteen-minute chat about it, does it count as a meeting? Not technically, though as a default, we still limit the ad hoc conversations we have on Thursdays. Fifteen minutes here and there throughout the day function the same as if you spent all day stuck in meetings.

The result is that we basically give the entire team one focus day each week, allowing us all to work on our biggest priorities and push them through to completion. You can choose any day of the week to be a no-meeting day, depending on what makes the most sense for your business team.

Energy and Attention: Who Has the Green Hat?

Sometimes the entire team will be working together to support a priority. Other times—particularly during high-priority events like product launches—it is helpful to give the person who's currently running with the ball the green hat.

I got this concept from Seth Godin, who originally (sometime before 2016) used the image of a red hat.[2] These days, red hats have a charged connotation; hence the color update. The point isn't the color of the hat or whether the hat even physically exists. The point is that sometimes you need to ask, "How do we as a team rally behind this one person and clear the lane so they can do their best work?"

In the military, if we refer to a unit as the main effort (or say it has priority of effort), it signifies to everyone that this unit gets anything it needs and everyone else's job is to support it. If you're capturing a beachhead, the team responsible for clearing the beach has the main priority because if that fails, the rest of the mission falls apart. Many sports teams have similar ways of indicating who has the primary effort—normally, the person with the ball.

In an office setting, when one teammate has the green hat, the rest of the team should give them space in their schedule. If a meeting comes up, ask twice if the person with the green hat really needs to be there for it. If you have a question or need help, think twice before pinging the person with the green hat.

How do you give someone the green hat?

Call It Out

During the planning process and meetings, include a prompt to ask who is making the main effort in each phase of a project. Then, create a daily habit that signifies who has the green hat that day. For example, when the person with the green hat comes into the office or checks in virtually, they can give a quick reminder to the rest of the team.

Own It

When you have the green hat, you shouldn't have to ask for permission to get out of things. If you're a soldier on guard detail and you're called to a meeting, you don't ask if it's okay for you to stay on guard duty. You stay on that detail until you're relieved. In the same way, you should keep that green hat until your piece is done—that's the whole point of prioritization. If people can't wait for the person with the green hat to finish their high-priority work before calling them to a meeting, the team is just running through the tyranny of the urgent.

Indicate the Transfer Point

Create time or milestone boundaries around the green hat. A team member should have the green hat either for a limited time or until they reach a milestone where they hand it off to the next person.

Report on Progress

Finally, have the person who's wearing the green hat report on everything they were able to accomplish because they were given that space. This reaffirms the value of the green-hat team habit and allows the person who was wearing the green hat to acknowledge that the rest of the team is covering shifts for them.

Finally, it gives the entire team visibility regarding the status quo with the green hat. It introduces the idea that maybe we can change the way we work together so that more of us can focus on our high-priority work. Maybe we could give the entire team the green hat from time to time.

Shout Out the Force Multipliers

I want to acknowledge that women and people of color often have a different relationship with wearing the green hat than white men do. Our society is largely built so that priority defaults to white men, so it can be incredibly energizing and empowering for women and people of color to wear the green hat.

But it can also come with a learning curve if you haven't been socialized to say no when other people ask for help. Some team members feel more awkward than others about sinking into the support that the team can provide. Some team members will benefit from better team habits around belonging so that they will believe they won't be diminished or reprimanded for asking for the support they need when they are making the main effort.

Race and gender aside, some people may have trouble wearing the green hat because they love playing the role of force multiplier and enabler on a team. These behind-the-scenes people are amazing, but our society and our work cultures typically do not reward them nearly as much as it rewards the heroes. While the green hat can be a useful tool for pushing forward priorities, its very existence should be a reminder that this is a team effort.

Be aware of your star players, and make sure to appreciate them for their contribution—and then ask them to step aside so you can acknowledge how everyone else contributed to making that happen. It's rarely the case that the star is some sort of superhuman alien who can do it all on their own. Usually, there are four or five other unsung heroes who have come together to achieve the goal.

Money: What's the Budget for This?

The final question you need to get in the habit of asking when it comes to new organizational or team priorities is "Are we creating a new budget to do this?" If the answer is yes, then the goal becomes a true priority. If you're not willing to carve out a budget to make this happen, you're unwilling to prioritize the goal.

Creating a new budget doesn't have to mean adding funds and resources to support the new priority. It could also mean removing something from someone's plate to reallocate an existing budget.

In a team setting, any change in activity costs money. Asking for time on someone's schedule is functionally equivalent to allocating funds to whatever is taking priority during that time. If you have no intention of creating an additional budget for a project you've already had several team meetings about, you've effectively spent thousands of dollars on the project already just in meeting costs.

When I point this out to clients, they often have an "Aha!" moment, quickly followed by frustration. All those meetings they've had about saving money or doing the project on the cheap—especially in a small business or nonprofit scenario—actually cost them a lot more money than if they'd just paid for the support they needed from the beginning.

This is obvious when I point it out but easy to overlook in the day-to-day, especially if you're not the one writing the paychecks. But meetings cost money. Emails cost money. Test procedure specification reports cost money. **If you're unwilling to create a budget for your project, you're unwilling to really see it forward.** So stop meeting about it, stop writing about it, and stop talking about it because you're just spending money on a goal you don't intend to see through.

For example, one of our team members is in charge of keyword research for our content. She had been cobbling together several different free tools and finally asked for a meeting to discuss upgrading to a paid account that would save her several hours per month.

The tool turned out to cost $99/year, which was far less than I was paying for her time each month. From her perspective, it made sense to spend more time rather than asking for a budget. From my perspective, I only have so many amazing humans on my team, and they have only so much time, energy, and attention available to them. It's relatively easy to make another $100 a year. It's much harder to find more hours in the day.

It's more difficult to ask the budget question when you're lower on the organizational ladder, but building a team habit of regularly analyzing the TEAM costs of your team's goals and projects gives everyone the language and tools to ensure that the team can actually prioritize the goals that have been set for them.

 **ROCKET PRACTICE**

MAKE GOALS PRIORITIES

» Define the TEAM cost for every goal:

1. Where will this goal live in the team's schedule? What days and focus blocks (see Chapter 10) will be used to push this effort through?

2. Who will own the main effort for what phases of this project? How will you indicate when a team member has the green hat? How specifically will the team clear the path to support their work?

3. What is the budget for this project? Remember to include resource needs and team time in that budget.

» What could you change about your team schedule to give everyone the green hat for an afternoon or even an entire day?

LEAVE ROOM FOR FAILURE

Many organizations either explicitly or implicitly have a zero tolerance for failure policy. On paper, this might make it seem like your success rate for goals will be higher than that of other organizations—but in reality, it means that your organization will have a harder time achieving *true* successes.

Why? Because people will quickly learn that it's best to sandbag their goals by choosing an easy goal they know they can accomplish. This keeps them from getting in trouble, but sandbagging is typically a team and individual coping strategy when the organization doesn't encourage growth—and the failure that comes with that growth.

When your team tries big things, there will be some slip-ups. There will be Crisco watermelons, or places where the project is dropped during handoff. If your sole goal as a manager, leader, or teammate is to avoid failure, then the individuals on your team will compensate by choosing goals for which they know they'll have zero failures.

They will not innovate. They will not risk anything. They will not try something new—and the end result will be that you will not achieve the true successes that will transform your team and your organization to the version they need to become next year. Instead, what you'll get is the team managing against last year's competencies and priorities.

This philosophy shows up in how an organization incentivizes performances. Are managers encouraged to eke out more profit by slashing team expenses rather than by increasing their value proposition? Are individuals rewarded for staying in their lane and punished when they bring new ideas to the table?

When your management or your organization incentivizes safe goals because there's no room for failure, your team will survive. Individuals will stay on the team. But the team—and the organization—will not be high performance.

In the book *Competing for the Future*, Gary Hamel and C. K. Prahalad[3] make the case that if your sole focus is on managing the denominator—keeping things tight and lean—your business will not be competitive. You have to focus on the numerator growth—new business lines, new revenue streams, more profit—in order to really grow your business. It's very difficult for most teams to manage the denominator and grow the numerator at the same time. And, unfortunately, in the same way that some organizations incentivize lower and safer goals, they also incentivize conservatism when it comes to managing the denominator instead of growing the numerator.

This includes the ways that organizations cultivate and retain the best people. If a teammate is meeting with their manager to talk about their future at an organization with a zero-failure policy, they'll chart a career path that doesn't stretch them. They won't take on the types of goals and roles that will stretch them, and they won't seek out the learning that will help them cultivate their skills and grow into the leaders the organization needs them to be.

ROCKET PRACTICE

MAKE ROOM FOR FAILURE

» How is failure approached within your team or organization? What would need to change about the goal incentive structure to make more room for people to bring new ideas to the table, take smart risks, and try big things?

CHAPTER 5 TAKEAWAYS

- Understanding how ready your team is to meet certain goals is key to setting goals they can actually accomplish.
- Focusing on improving a team's habits is one of the fastest ways to reach a higher readiness level.
- Humans choose which goals to advance based on a number of nonrational factors, including pain, reward, ease, gamification, and values.
- Convert push goals (external motivations) into pull goals (internal motivations) whenever possible.
- Prioritizing a goal requires allocating TEAM (time, energy, attention, and money) costs.
- If you haven't left room for failure, you will never create space for your team to achieve real success.

SIX

PLANNING

Planning defines the particular place you
want to be and how you intend to get there.
It's a responsibility rather than a technique.

—Frances Hesselbein

In the *South Park* episode "Gnomes,"[1] the titular gnomes unveil a business plan consisting of Phase 1: Collect underpants; Phase 2: ?; Phase 3: Profit. In *Start Finishing*, I call this Phase 2 question mark the "air sandwich," a term I adapted from Nilofer Merchant. And often when I'm brought in to help a company troubleshoot why things aren't working, I find it's because there was a problem with the plan.

If the last few chapters on decision-making, goal-setting, and prioritization were about answering the questions "Where are we, and where are we trying to go?," planning is about asking the question "How will we get there?"

Yet for many organizations, planning (and communication, which we'll discuss in the next chapter) are left as big question marks. They become the air sandwich in between strategy and execution. But you have to have a plan. You have to communicate that plan. And you have to follow up on that plan in order to push it forward.

For the rest of this chapter, we'll dig into the team habits that turn poor plans into great plans. But first, let's address the objection I can already hear some of you starting to make: "This is great, Charlie, but I'm just an individual contributor. I'm not the one who's supposed to come up with the plan."

If that's the case, the first team habit shift you need to make is to understand that **planning is everyone's job.**

MAKE PLANNING EVERYONE'S JOB

When you have a great plan, it's invisible. Your team is all on the same page, no one is confused, and everything just works. A great plan is something the team runs *with*, not runs *into*.

And that's part of what makes planning so tricky. It's pretty easy to know you have a planning problem when things are going wrong, but just because you have a high-performing team—a team that is just rocking and rolling along with their amazing plan—doesn't mean you have good team planning habits.

More likely, it means there's a great planner behind the scenes who's doing a fantastic job of strategizing and communicating. Often, this one person is laying the entire bedrock for the team to do great work together, and the rest of the team doesn't realize that their key to successful planning is tied up in a single role until it's too late.

You don't want a single point of failure in any team. If you've built a habit around one person being good at planning, inevitably, that person will need a break. That person will be pulled into different things. That person likely has a job outside their planning duties. That's why, as much as possible, planning should be a distributed core function of the team.

In smaller companies, the planner is typically the founder—and Productive Flourishing is no exception. I'm very good at planning, and I've been trained for it from some of my earliest roles. When I'm in the room with the rest of my team, plans are made faster. They're tighter. But for the sake of the team, we don't want it to be the case that only Charlie knows how to make the plan.

To avoid that, we have made planning a core skill within the company. We specifically train individual team members to create their portion of every plan, and one of the ways you grow at Productive Flourishing is to take on ever larger planning and management projects.

When someone at the company has an idea, they're in charge of coming up with a back-of-the-napkin plan to get the ball rolling. I say, "Let's flesh that out. What's the revenue model? What resources will it take to pull this off? What's the timeline? What will it displace? How many units of time will you need to shift over to this idea? What's the cost per unit?"

Every time I make a new plan, I use it as an opportunity to include my team in the process, to model my approach, and to remind them that ideas don't get off the ground without a plan. It's worth taking the time to learn how to plan well and teach the skill to others on your team.

 **ROCKET PRACTICE**

TEACH EVERY TEAM MEMBER HOW TO PLAN

» Is one person on your team typically in charge of the planning process? What can be done to expand the planning process by asking individual team members to own the planning step for their own parts of the project?

» What templates, checklists, or resources can your team create to help facilitate the planning process and make it easier for new team members to practice the skill?

POOR PLANNING PRODUCES POOR PERFORMANCE

If you've served in the military, you might have heard of the "7Ps," which for the sake of the business audience I'll clean up and call the 5Ps: Poor

Planning Produces Poor Performance. The phrase is self-explanatory, but that's the thing about rocket practice. Just because we know we should be planning doesn't mean we plan well—or at all.

So what makes a plan?

1. **Goal.** A specified goal of what's trying to be achieved.
2. **Timeline.** A defined timeline during which you'll execute the plan.
3. **People.** A specific allocation of the *right* people to accomplish said plan.
4. **Commitment.** A commitment to sharing, referencing, and updating the plan.

I want to slow down on this last point for a minute because it's critical and yet is still somehow the most overlooked step. You may have done a pretty good job of planning, but you're not using the plan. It's almost worse than if you didn't plan at all. Here's why.

Not Sharing the Plan

One of my jobs after returning from overseas was to plan joint training exercises between the Air Force, the Army, and some of our foreign allies. I would run teams through tactical maneuver scenarios—basically, they had to deliver supplies through a scenario that we would set up. On the flip side, I trained teams in how to assault and ambush convoys. Everyone had fun—except for those in the convoys that were being ambushed.

That was because our convoy commanders lost most of the time. My job as a trainer was to remind them that they *will* lose most of the time if they don't pay attention to a few key things. Two of those basics were:

1. Make sure that the convoy commander and assistant convoy commander aren't in the same vehicle.
2. Share the plan with the rest of the team before going in.

The problem was that it takes time to properly come up with and communicate a plan, and inevitably, convoy commanders and assistant convoy commanders would rush. In the interest of time, they would often just get into the same vehicle without having shared their plan with the rest of the group.

The command vehicle was typically the Humvee with two antennas sticking out of the top; of course, I trained the convoy assault teams to look for those two antennas. And when the command vehicle was taken out in the middle of these scenarios, the rest of the convoy almost always shut down.

Why? The rest of the unit might have been given a rough plan, but it didn't go into detail about certain questions: What happens when the commander and assistant commander are taken out? Who takes charge? Where are we going? What's the objective? How do you lead a recovery operation?

The mission failed because it was operating on a ghost plan.

Sometimes, one or two individuals on the team get together and come up with a strong plan, and because they're working so quickly they forget to share it with the rest of the group.

These ghost plans are one of the most insidious causes of friction and frustration in a team because the people with the ghost plan are frustrated that no one else is on board, and the people who aren't in the know can sense it—but they don't know what to do about it.

Now, most of us aren't in a combat scenario or dealing with a trainer who won't pull punches. But in the day-to-day battlefield of business, our leaders might be taken out of commission when they go on vacation or are stuck in meetings. You need to make sure the plan is shared, or the rest of the effort comes to a grinding halt.

Not Referencing the Plan

You sat down as a team and set a clear course of action. You probably even documented it somewhere. Everyone left the meeting with a solid idea of what they're meant to do next. Great, right?

Only one problem. If that meeting was the last time you ever talked about the plan, it's almost as bad as if you didn't make it in the first place. Even in the most aligned team, individual team members will all have personalized ideas of what the plan is, and those ideas increasingly become adrift from the original plan as time passes if you don't have a team habit of referencing the plan.

This is often caused by the human pattern of addition. In the book *Subtract: The Untapped Science of Less*,[2] Leidy Klotz points out that as humans, we have a bias to add things instead of subtract. When his son surprised him by solving a Lego puzzle by removing a block rather than adding one (as Klotz had planned to do), he began carrying that same Lego structure around to ask colleagues how they would solve it. Nearly all chose the solution that required more bricks rather than taking bricks away.

This realization set off a series of experiments that reinforced Klotz's theory that humans are inclined to find solutions that require adding *more* to a project, even when they are financially incentivized to subtract.

One of the first things a great editor or writer will do to make a piece of writing more clear is to slash unnecessary phrases, sentences, and even entire paragraphs. A novice writer, on the other hand, will often think they need to write more to get their point across.

The same thing happens with plans. If the plan isn't 100 percent clear to everyone, our natural tendency is to solve that problem by adding *more*. You and I will both try to fill in a gap, but if we're not referencing the original plan, we're probably adding different things.

The purpose of a plan isn't just for us all to be aligned at the beginning but also to keep us on track as we go. Pull that plan back up in meetings. Reference it when scheduling deadlines and daily tasks. And anytime you reference it, notice if you've subconsciously added a new constraint or assumption. Is it unnecessary? Get rid of it. Is it helpful? Update the plan.

Not Updating the Plan

Whenever we make a plan, we do so with the information available at the time. As we execute that plan, new information, new constraints, and new priorities will arise. If we don't continuously update the plan with those new pieces, we'll end up with some teammates working with the new information and assumptions (which exist only in their own minds) while others are still working from the old plan.

You essentially have two different teams working on two different sets of goals, plans, and outcomes.

The reason this is worse than not planning at all is that if you didn't have a plan, you'd at least have to keep checking in with each other about what is going on. **Having a plan that hasn't been updated means everyone *thinks* they know what's going on, but no one actually has the full picture.**

I see a lot of teams using the habit of daily standups to keep people on the same page. On the surface, it makes sense to kick off every day with a ten-minute check-in to align priorities and dispense new information. In reality, daily standups can contribute to poor planning for two reasons.

First, the standup becomes a crutch that substitutes for good planning because it becomes acceptable to shoot from the hip every day. Crutch meetings, as we'll discuss in Chapter 9, are a very expensive way to solve a planning problem.

Second, the standup has a tendency to produce a lot of new information that rarely is captured in the original plan. If everyone is present at every standup, this isn't a huge problem. But people are out sick. They travel. They have other priorities that cause them to miss a meeting, and when they walk back into work a week later and look at the plan, they'll have no idea what's actually going on.

ROCKET PRACTICE

GET EVERYONE ON THE SAME PAGE

» How are plans shared after they're made? Who owns communicating the plan to everyone who needs to know it? (Don't just leave this up to "someone"!)

» Is the plan written down in an accessible location where everyone on the team can easily reference it? How frequently does your team revisit the plan? What mechanisms are in place to ensure that the team is referencing the plan regularly?

» What is the process of updating the plan? How are plan updates communicated to teammates who may not have been present when a decision to update the plan was made?

CREATE A TIMELINE

One of the ways to look at a plan is that it's **an idea or goal situated on a timeline**. We spent the whole last chapter talking about how to set better goals, so now let's talk about timelines.

A poor plan may have intent, but without a timeline, it doesn't go anywhere. On the flip side, if you have a timeline with no real sense of the intent or destination, no one on the team knows what they're working toward. Both pieces of the equation are equally important when it comes to planning.

What makes a good timeline? Ask yourself these questions.

Who Are the Different Stakeholders Who Need to See the Timeline, and How Granular Do They Need the Timeline to Be?

One of the big challenges for teams—especially across multiple levels—is that the timeline needs to reflect different horizons and granularity depending on the audience.

- Leaders: quarterly, yearly, multiyear
- Managers: monthly, quarterly
- Individual contributors: weekly, daily

If you have too many dates and times cluttering up a yearly or multi-year timeline, it's hard for leaders who are planning at that level to see the overall architecture of the goal. On the flip side, if you have too broad an intent—for example, just a deadline at the end of the quarter with no milestones along the way—then it's next to impossible for individual contributors to tell whether they're on track.

A good timeline needs to keep the audience in mind and be specific enough to keep the project on track without getting lost into too much granularity.

Does the Timeline Adequately Account for Rework Margin and Slack?

The other place that plans go wrong is when teams are filled to 100 percent capacity. Imagine you have eight hours to work each day. Planning to use every minute of those eight hours doesn't leave you any margin for error; there's no time for last-minute meetings, fixing mistakes, or doing work that takes longer than expected. And I can guarantee that all of those things will come up, regardless of the time you've allowed in your schedule for them.

Here's where the 85 Percent Rule can help: When planning, only ever fill your team's capacity to 85 percent.

Following that rule means assuming that for every eight-hour day, you should plan for just shy of seven hours of work. If something comes up (which it inevitably will), that leaves the team with enough capacity to handle it while still staying on track with the work that's already on their plates.

Of course, where people run into trouble with the 85 Percent Rule is in assuming that their team has a blank slate to work with. That's why you need to ask the following.

How Does the Timeline Relate to Priority Timelines across the Rest of the Team and the Organization?

Whether in our personal lives or in our teams (where this effect is amplified), when we sit down to plan a project, we often treat it as if it were the only thing on our plate. We estimate how long it will take to do it without remembering that this project will be stacked on top of all the other things that we're doing.

The timeline might look great—until you remember all the other priorities across your team. Those priorities aren't always other big strategic projects. In fact, most teams run into trouble by forgetting just how much recurring work is on their plate every week and underestimating the extent to which urgent work takes up their attention.

In reality, if you're like most teams I've worked with, you're probably spending 50–60 percent of your time on recurring projects. If a new project will require 50 percent of your team's time, you will have to remove some recurring work from their plates so that the new project will not become yet another strategic-routine-urgent logjam (which we'll talk about in a moment).

Are the Milestones Clear Enough That the Team Knows When One Is Done?

Great project managers know that projects get wobbly when you have a milestone or deadline but it's not clear what "done" looks like. One person might think they've finished a task, but when they hand it off, the person who receives the baton has to go back to them and say, "Your part of this isn't done yet."

Often, this is less about the individual's inability to do the work than about the clarity of what work needs to be done and what target needs to be hit.

What Are the Key Dates and Milestones That Need to Be Explicitly Communicated?

Different communication triggers should be built into the timeline in order to keep people on the team—and across the organization, if applicable—abreast of progress. This is often the job of whoever is playing the coordinator role on the team, which we'll talk about in more depth in the chapter on collaboration.

Incorporating an update cadence into the plan helps keep the work on track while reducing the emotional load and anxiety of key stakeholders and teammates who may be wondering what's going on.

Projects can sometimes end up in a frustrating cycle where the team spends more time explaining where things are than pushing the work forward. The more they can preemptively communicate milestones to key stakeholders, the more likely it is that they will be left alone to do the work rather than explaining the status of the work.

It's very hard for a team to respond nondefensively when someone asks for an update. Even if the plan is on track, they know they're hearing the question because someone has been left out of the loop.

For instance, my team knows that if I don't hear something about a project after about two weeks, I will ask about it. They don't have to check in every day unless it's a high-priority project leading up to a launch. But if I haven't heard anything for a while, I will ask about it because I know that if I care about the project being completed, I need to keep the heat on it.

If you say you'll communicate on Friday, and by Monday I still haven't heard from you, then I'll worry. But if you touch base on Friday and say, "X, Y, and Z happened, and I'll get this to you Monday or Tuesday," then you're good.

When it comes to timelines, too many people underconsider those communication milestones and the cadence that needs to be incorporated without becoming overly obsessive about capturing every task.

MAKE BETTER TIMELINES

» Review how your team creates and shares timelines by asking yourself these questions about your timeline:

1. Who are the different stakeholders who need to see the timeline, and how granular do they need the timeline to be?

2. Does the timeline adequately account for rework margin and slack?

3. How does the timeline relate to priority timelines across the rest of the team and the organization?

4. Are the milestones clear enough that the team knows when one is done?

5. What are the key dates and milestones that need to be explicitly communicated?

» What's one element that needs to be added to your team's timeline habits that would make a significant difference to their ability to stay aligned on a project? On the flip side, what's one major element that needs to be subtracted to help your team stay aligned with the project?

» Where are previous plans and timelines documented so that you can review them when making the next timeline in order to become even better at capturing what needs to happen on what timeline?

AVOID STRATEGIC-ROUTINE-URGENT LOGJAMS

Is your team caught in a cycle of logjams between your strategic, routine, and urgent work?

- **Strategic work:** work that is longer term and catalytic for an important objective or issue in the organization

- **Routine work:** tasks that pop up regularly, such as weekly reports
- **Urgent work:** time-sensitive and important tasks

Logjams happen when the last-minute work becomes standard and the strategic work falls by the wayside. We begin to vacillate between doing what's urgent and then tackling the routine work while we're catching our breath before the next urgent thing happens. The strategic work doesn't have the same time sensitivity as the urgent and routine work, which means it won't be attended to until it becomes urgent.

Here are a few planning rules that can help reduce those logjams.

The One-Third–Two-Thirds Rule

Most Crisco watermelons (see Chapter 3) and efforts that require Dunkirk spirit (Chapter 5) occur because either someone didn't create a plan or they took way too long to create an overly detailed, overly rigorous plan that left the team with too little time and flexibility to actually execute it. It may seem like no big deal, but the two- to three-day rushes that happen when plans aren't delivered quickly can displace two to three weeks of work.

If you allow your team enough time and flexibility that they don't need to create a full-on displacement of work to finish new projects, you will cause less downstream disruption of other projects and work the team might be doing, meaning fewer strategic-routine-urgent logjams.

That's where the One-Third–Two-Thirds Rule comes in. The One-Third–Two-Thirds Rule states that you should spend one-third of the total time planning and allow two-thirds of the time for your team to complete the project. If the deadline is the end of the quarter, for example, you should spend no more than a month in the planning phase. If the timeline is nine months, don't spend more than three months planning.

One of the reasons we hold on to plans as long as we often do is that we're concerned the team will be frustrated if we change things along the way. Most people would rather have more time, knowing there may be pivots, than scramble to do their work at the last minute.

Commit:Complete Ratio

Your commit:complete ratio is a very simple concept that has a very powerful outcome. For every project you commit to, how many do you complete?

Let's say your commit:complete ratio is 50 percent. For every new project your team takes on, you all fundamentally know whether you'll succeed is a fifty-fifty shot—which can be demoralizing and makes it hard to commit the necessary time and resources to planning.

If your commit:complete ratio is in the 70–80 percent range, that starts to feel pretty good. As a team, we understand that challenges might arise—changing priorities, urgent work, a VUCA environment, and other things that are out of our control. But we at least believe that we're capable of pushing projects through to the end.

Having a commit:complete ratio of 100 percent may sound good on paper, but it actually is an indication that your team is performing below their true level of capabilities.

As we discussed in the chapter on goal-setting, when you only pick projects you know your team can achieve, you don't take moon shots. You don't truly innovate. You don't tap into the full depth of your people's latent talent, which means that your teammates may not be as fulfilled and energized by the work they *are* doing.

Now, obviously, if you're a doctor or a NASA engineer or a military commander or someone in a similar field, we want you to have a success rate that's near 100 percent. But for the rest of us who work in scenarios where people's lives don't depend on us, the sweet spot for a commit:complete ratio is in that 70–80 percent band. In that range, your team has the confidence to tackle difficult, challenging work and succeed, which increases belonging and rapport as well as their capacity to choose more audacious goals.

To use this ratio, start tracking what you've actually committed to. I recommend tracking projects that are week-sized or more. After a month or so, take a look at how many of these projects you've managed to push across the finish line.

Before you share that number with the rest of your team, ask them to guess what it is. You're not looking for a right or wrong answer; this isn't a political moment where you're trying to make a point. (Because of this, it can be helpful to have the guesses be submitted in secret.) This acts as a temperature check for how the team feels about their own success rate.

Next, use your commit:complete ratio as a springboard for reality-check conversations about which projects you might struggle to complete. This helps your team have a premortem about why or why not they're likely to struggle with this particular project. Is it more complex than people think it is? Is it tied to a core capacity that the team doesn't have? Is it one that—given the rest of your workload—you know will be routinely deprioritized? Is it something the team just doesn't want to do, so it will require extra motivation to get it done?

The more your team has these premortem conversations, the more you will develop a sense of which projects will require a bit more attention and an ability to commit adequate resources to projects.

The point isn't to use this commit:complete ratio as an excuse to back down from particularly challenging projects. **Knowing your commit:complete ratio gives you the language and tools to perform a reality check on important projects so you can commit the necessary resources to get them done.**

The 3x Rule

The strategic part of the strategic-routine-urgent triad is one of the hardest parts to nail down. It's difficult to specify the timeline for strategic work, and the outcomes are sometimes unclear. Even if you do think you know how hard a project will be before you start, strategic work is almost always more difficult, more time-consuming, and more complex than you think it will be.

After all, if strategic work was easy, it would already be done.

Some of the thorniest problems in business take a long time to work through because they are multipronged and multidimensional. That's why I tell clients to use the 3x Rule and **assume that strategic**

work will be three times more intensive than they initially think it would be.

When planning for bigger projects, give yourself and your team three times as much time as you think will be needed. This more accurately reflects the effort that will actually be required and helps you build in the margin that will allow you to do better strategic work as opposed to just delivering in a time crunch.

The Five Projects Rule

The last planning tool is the Five Projects Rule, which is that you should have no more than five active projects on your plate per time horizon (i.e., day, week, month, quarter, or year). When I teach this rule to individuals, I usually say that of the five projects you can have on your plate, only three can be work projects; the other two should be life projects. For teams, think of "life" projects as things like meetings or admin.

This becomes tricky when you start thinking about how those three remaining projects relate to the strategic-routine-urgent triad. In an ideal world, one of those projects is routine or recurring work. For example, every August at Productive Flourishing, we do our back-to-school and back-to-work campaigns. It's not a surprise when August rolls around and this particular batch of work needs done. It might look a little different every year, but we expect it and have planned for it in our yearly schedule.

As I write this, in August, we're also working on the launch of our Momentum app, which is a big push that takes up quite a bit of our time. We also have some urgent work on our plate because we're switching email marketing systems, and we know that needs to be done soon because we have a rule about not switching any systems right before a launch. (If you've been around the block more than once, you probably know why that rule exists.)

That's three big projects that Team PF is tackling right now, one of which is routine and two of which are urgent. Where is the strategic work getting done? When are we roadmapping new features for the Momentum app or working on our next product—a book called *Team Habits* that I hope you'll be holding in your hands at some point in the future?

What we do is clarify the trade-offs we're making and make our peace with them. Doing so requires clear communication about the work that's already on your plate and why you can or cannot take on a new project—or defining what you can eliminate in order to take on new work.

At Team PF, we do this by putting projects through a cage match during our planning sessions:

- **List** the projects that are on the table. (Don't forget recurring or routine projects—seeing them through requires *time, energy, and attention.*)
- **Compare** the relative strength and pull of each project with others, and eliminate those that obviously will not make it.
- **Choose** a project that seems strong and compare it to the other projects remaining in the match. Which ones does it beat? Which one beats it?
- **Rinse and repeat** until you achieve a rough sense of the order of project strengths.
- **Assess** what made the projects particularly strong, starting from the top project and working your way down.

Recurring work is usually a good candidate for elimination in a project cage match, whether you're working on a small entrepreneurial team or in a large corporation. It's common for people to figure out how to become more efficient so they can make room for more on their plates. It's courageous for them to speak up and say, "We don't have the bandwidth for this. What will we eliminate in order to get that work done?"

Just because routine work has been done for the last six years doesn't mean it needs to stay on your team's plate today.

**ROCKET PRACTICE**

CLEAR THE LOGJAMS

» Based on your goal date for completion, set a deadline for the planning phase that is no more than one-third of the total project time. Ask what is the bare minimum information your team needs to get started, and how—and when—will the rest of the plan be communicated?

» Calculate your commit:complete ratio and get in the habit of having premortem conversations when new projects come up. Are there particular projects that the team tends to struggle with or that need a bit more attention to be pushed across the finish line?

» Is there enough room in the team's schedule to take on strategic work, or is their schedule filled with urgent and recurring work? Take a look at all the routine tasks and projects that are filling your team's plate. Ask the following:

1. Can we eliminate it? Would it make any difference if we did?

2. Can we continue intentionally deferring recurring tasks without causing urgent or strategic harm?

3. Can we outsource the task or offload it to another team or function?

4. Can we be smarter and more efficient about the task?

CELEBRATE THE VOICE OF NO

Nobody likes to be told no—especially visionaries and creative folks who thrive on coming up with grandiose plans. When the brainstorming session is going well and the energy is high, the last thing a team wants is for someone to raise their hand and say, "I get that you all are excited about this, but here's why it's not going to work."

The Voice of No is a critical part of any team planning session. It might seem like a downer, but we really need to celebrate the Voice of

No, because every plan needs constraints. It needs someone who really believes in it *and* who is also willing to point out the flaws.

This is another reason I appreciate my military training, because in the military, there are people whose job it is to poke holes in a plan in order to make it more sound. Their job is to say, "That's great, but what happens if X, Y, or Z? Let's scenario-plan that." That's what the Voice of No does.

Now, I'm not talking about devil's advocates—the devil doesn't need any more advocates. **But every team does need a Voice—or Voices—of No whose job it is to ask about scope creep, to ask whether we really need that addition to the plan, to ask whether that timeline seems realistic, and to ask about changing priorities.**

In fact, I like to think of it more as wearing the No Hat rather than having one person always being the Voice of No. The role should flip around the team, so when it's your job to voice concerns, you can see how much work it actually is. You can see how much courage it takes to look at a person or people you believe in, who are so excited about a project, and say, "I hear you. And there are a few things we need to think about first, so let's slow down just a little bit."

The Voice of No doesn't have to be Eeyore, the pessimistic, gloomy stuffed donkey from *Winnie-the-Pooh*. They can be gregarious. They can be extroverted. They can be excited about the project *and* be willing to ask tough questions like "We seem to be overcommitted already. What are we going to give up to make this happen?"

As a strategic consultant or executive coach, I am often the Voice of No.

In his book *Six Thinking Hats*,[3] Edward de Bono points out that the Black Hat (which is used to point out risks, difficulties, and problems) is probably the most powerful hat. Rather than being the voice of doom, the Black Hat has evolved from our human sense of danger and survival instinct. "The Black Hat is the basis of Western Civilization," de Bono writes, "because the Black Hat is the basis of critical thinking."

The reason that I use the term "Voice of No" is because I want us all to change the valence of the word "No." It shouldn't be a bad word;

instead, it should act as an affirmation about what's important to us and what our values and priorities are.

As Harvard Business School professor Michael Porter said, "The essence of strategy is deciding what not to do."[4]

The Voice of No can be an incredible champion for a team's resources, priorities, strategy, belonging, and so on. Which means we need to empower that voice and embrace it, but we also need to spread that energy around so that everyone feels empowered to have the courage to speak up.

Be aware that the Voice of No can also be useful when it is brought to goal-setting. Is it realistic to triple our business over the next year? Is it realistic that we'll be able to launch all those new products on that timeline? Those are all questions the Voice of No should be asking.

 ROCKET PRACTICE

DESIGNATE A VOICE OF NO

» Does one teammate tend to be the Voice of No during the planning process? What could be changed in how their tough questions are asked or in the way the team receives the feedback? How can your team better celebrate that person's contributions?

» What could be changed in your team to give more people the opportunity to speak up when they spot a potential challenge?

NORMALIZE THAT PLANS ARE MADE TO BE CHANGED

Some people have the mindset that if you create a plan, it's chiseled in stone. Maybe it's their personality to want specificity and rigor, or maybe they don't trust that the team can think on their feet.

In reality, most plans are obsolete almost as soon as you start making them. New information and priorities arise, and new conditions develop. If your planning process is overly long because you're trying to come up with the perfect plan, this creates two problems. First, it causes so much delay that by the time the plan is finished, the conditions have changed. Second, it creates a sunk cost fallacy where you've invested so much time in the plan that you have even more resistance to change.

It turns out that in most domains, the best planners are those who change their plans most frequently. The teams that can use a plan as a guideline for action are usually more effective than those that use it as an unalterable instruction manual.

In Chapter 2, I mentioned the Army principle of collecting information by action, aka doing stuff and seeing what happens. The teams that end up winning more often than not are those that embrace the philosophy of doing stuff to see what happens and then updating their plan accordingly.

This might seem to counter the advice I gave in the last chapter about sticking with goals for the entire cycle rather than constantly changing them. That advice still stands; however, you should be adjusting the *plan* for how to reach that goal as you go.

Adaptive planning isn't as wasteful as many hard-core planners think. When you adopt the mindset that plans are made to be changed, it has the following benefits.

- It breaks the cycle of overplanning and meetings followed by more meetings to create an overly detailed plan that will become obsolete by the next meeting.
- It prevents unnecessary work because the team learns to adapt to new conditions as opposed to just following the plan headlong even though conditions have changed.
- It requires the team to learn better adaptive communication and real-time collaboration because they're forced to think on their feet and work together.
- It helps the team learn to identify essential guiding principles rather than being distracted by extraneous data.

In an ideal world, plans would be designed to be adaptive from the top down. The top layer of the plan would consist of guiding information and parameters but not much detail. The managerial layer would add more robustness and guidance. And the bottom layer, with the individual contributors, would contain the densest information because they're the ones who are working at the ground level.

In the real world, the inverse is often the case. The higher levels of the plan tend to have too much information, which doesn't leave room for the managerial and individual contributor layers to add their voices and insights to how to best execute the plan. This makes the top layer not only bloated and hard to follow but also often incorrect because the people making the plan at that level aren't the ones actually doing the work.

In some situations and industries, you do need plans that are overengineered from top to bottom. If you're a NASA engineer, you're designing medical equipment, or you're a civil engineer building bridges, you might need books and books of governing scenarios that cover different use cases. But most of us live in a world where a wide margin of error can exist without causing catastrophe, and our teams could stand to think a little more on their feet.

Project Status Scorecards

One way to keep track of a plan as it changes is through the use of scorecards to indicate progress toward project milestones. These could be tags in your project management tool or spreadsheet.

- **Green:** The project is on track and within parameters or accomplished.
- **Yellow:** We're still within a range of acceptability here, but we need to pay attention.
- **Red:** We're offtrack or have come up against a block that needs to be addressed.

Red scorecards are an indication that there's trouble and should be seen as an invitation to work together to solve the problem. But all too often, teams have set up the scorecard system so that no one can use red. Red scorecards are treated as huge problems, and the teammates who point them out can find themselves under fire for doing so.

If we stick with the assumptions about our teammates that we started this book with—that we're all inherently goal-oriented, relationship-minded, completion-motivated, and doing our best—then we can also assume that if someone has flipped over the red scorecard on a project, they've probably done as much as they can to push things forward. They've exhausted either their team resources or mental resources, and it's time to have an open conversation about what you can do as a team to support or unblock them.

In the chapter on goal-setting, we talked about how team cultures that leave no room for failure will have a harder time achieving true successes. In the same way, if in your team culture no one can use a red scorecard without attracting negative attention or getting their tail chewed out, the rest of the scorecard system becomes meaningless. Problems won't surface until far too late in the process, when it's much harder to do anything to fix them.

ROCKET PRACTICE

CREATE MORE FLEXIBLE PLANS

» If you're struggling with letting go of hard-core planning, think about the macrostructure of the plan. What are the nonnegotiable guardrails that need to be locked down in the top level? What guidance will keep things on track at the managerial level to help see the plan through? And what technical details need to be added—or more likely subtracted—at the implementation level so that the people doing the work can have the autonomy to move the plan forward without wearing a straitjacket?

» How will you indicate whether the plan is on track? What needs to be changed to make it more acceptable for teammates to show yellow or red scorecards and ask for support?

CHAPTER 6 TAKEAWAYS

- Planning should be everyone's job. Build team habits that develop every teammate's planning skills.
- A plan consists of the following:
  - **Goal.** A specified goal of what you're trying to achieve.
  - **Timeline.** A defined timeline during which you'll execute the plan.
  - **People.** A specific allocation of the *right* people to accomplish said plan.
  - **Commitment.** A commitment to sharing, referencing, and updating the plan.
- To avoid strategic-routine-urgent logjams, follow the One-Third–Two-Thirds Rule, the 3x Rule, and the Five Projects Rule and know your commit:complete ratio.
- Every team needs a Voice—or Voices—of No who can ask the difficult questions about how the plan will succeed.
- Plans are made to be changed; when you plan to adapt, you'll be more prepared to handle the inevitable challenges that will arise.

SEVEN COMMUNICATION

*The two words "information" and "communication"
are often used interchangeably, but they signify
quite different things. Information is giving out;
communication is getting through.*

—SYDNEY J. HARRIS

When a banger comes on the radio while you're driving, you reach for the dial to turn it up. When your friend or spouse in the passenger seat wants to have a conversation, you turn the dial down. Too little bass? Too much treble? A few simple adjustments can help you achieve the exact right levels on the stereo to make your tunes (or podcast) sound fantastic, which makes your drive go more smoothly—whether you're on a weeklong road trip or a grocery run.

In the same way, you can turn the dials on your team's communication levels to achieve optimal clarity.

Most teams fall into a few broad patterns when it comes to how they communicate. Too much in one direction, and you create a bunch of unnecessary noise. Too little, and it's a recipe for confusion. Think of these patterns like the volume, fade, balance, and equalizer on your car stereo. As you audit your team according to the following communication patterns, keep in mind that—just as with your car stereo—you may need to adjust more than one dial in order to get the best sound.

TOO FREQUENT OR TOO INFREQUENT?

Attention is the scarcest resource your teammates have. If you're communicating too frequently, you're making too many claims on someone's attention without it being worth their time. This will eventually cause your teammates to make a Faustian bargain: Do they know what's in every CC Thread from Hell or Slack notification, or do they let updates slide and focus on their most important work?

Most people tend to figure out that if they ship their best work, it makes up for not being 100 percent in the know. Or, they find out the hard way that being in the know but not shipping work isn't enough to keep their jobs. I tend to lean toward people doing their most important work, but in some organizations, not being in the know can be grounds for performance write-ups—regardless of the work people are actually doing.

On the flip side, you may be communicating too infrequently, which means people are constantly uncertain about whether they have the most up-to-date information. A good way to gauge this is to consider how many of your team's communications are initiated by requests for updates. If you've set the "frequency" dial to the right level, your teammates and managers shouldn't have to waste energy constantly tracking down information or wading through mountains of emails and notifications to find out what's important.

TOO MUCH OR TOO LITTLE DETAIL?

If you've turned the "how much detail" dial up too high, that normally shows up in two ways. On the one hand, you run the risk of being so prescriptive about how people should do their work that you limit their ability to add their own genius. People can't do anything but follow the requirements you set, which can lead to lackluster work or a demoralized team that feels that they don't have the autonomy to do their jobs. On the other hand, the sheer volume of words and detail means that some people might just tune out instructions. They don't have time to sift through a wall of text or a thirty-minute monologue to figure out what's relevant to them, so they use their own best judgment and miss the guardrails you were trying to set up for them.

In full transparency, this is an area where I struggle as a leader. I like to give team members options for solving a scenario: a default way and two or three alternatives they can try if the default doesn't work.

If you've worked with me for a while, you understand I'm giving you a range of choices to help you work your own way through the problem. If you're new to the team, you might receive that wall of text and think, "Uh-oh, now I really don't know what to do because Charlie gave me three different directions." I've had to force myself to become very clear about which details are the priority.

On the other side of the dial, you can communicate too little detail. Visionary leaders and senior managers can be very bad about this. They communicate broad intent and vision when what their team really needs is parameters and details. Their instinct is to paint a picture of how the next three years are going to go when a teammate is just trying to figure out what to prioritize for next week.

Note that communicating too little detail can look a lot like communicating too infrequently. Here's one way to tell the difference: If your teammates constantly feel out of the loop or they're persistently working from last week's or last month's plan, it's probably because plan updates are being communicated too infrequently. If it seems that the team is always making bad decisions, they probably don't have enough informational detail to make tighter ones.

TOO FOCUSED OR TOO BROAD?

There's an art to knowing when your communication is too focused or too broad, and that's to understand the level of the problem you're trying to solve. As the saying goes, "Don't create global solutions for local problems." Some issues have a broad reach, and you have to solve them at that level rather than focusing on all the specific instances that have popped up. Others are purely local, and it would be a mistake to use a specific local problem to create a general rule or policy change that affects everyone.

One place where too much focus shows up is when senior-level executives are trying to solve deep technical problems. They shouldn't be spending their time or energy on something so specific; they should be putting their energy into solving more overarching problems and leaving this focus level of communication to the people whose job it is.

On the other hand, communicating too broadly about a topic means giving vague, general answers anytime someone brings up a specific problem.

Tuning the dial of too focused or too broad invites us as teammates, no matter our role, to ask what problem level we're dealing with. Are we drawing a general solution for a one-off problem, or are we ignoring a broader pattern that's actually a global problem because of our myopic focus?

TOO AFRAID OR TOO COURAGEOUS?

Far too many teams and organizations develop communication patterns that require them to dance around the edge of what they're really trying to say, which adds extra cognitive, emotional, and social load to the team dynamic. Why? Because speaking the truth requires courage in the best of team cultures; in the more toxic ones, speaking the truth is actively disincentivized.

To take a common example, it takes courage to say, "I know we're excited about this project, but I'm not sure we have the resources to meet that goal." That's why, if a team member is concerned, they might approach the subject from the side as a question: "Have we thought about what resources we need to reach that goal?"

This approach is often meant to invite conversation, which it absolutely can do. It is also easy to sweep it under the rug. Rather than approaching the problem directly and creating a useful conversation that can guide the team, the indirect approach dramatically increases the amount of work that it takes for a team to figure out what is actually being asked.

As my good friend Todd Sattersten said in a keynote speech, "Clarity requires courage."[1] When we are in the throes of being too afraid, it's hard for us to create the clarity of communication that the team needs to drive forward.

If we're sticking with the metaphor of the dial, there must be a setting for "Too courageous," right? The answer is that it's possible, but so many people, teams, and company cultures err on the side of being too afraid that I've almost never seen the courage dial turned up to 11.

Of course, fear-based communication can sometimes masquerade as too courageous. **Some teams develop the toxic habit of running at each other with knives under the pretense of having honest conversations.** There's a difference between having radically candid conversations where everyone is open to speak their truth and hurtfully airing grievances and calling it "courageous conversation." That type of conversation is still fear based, but instead of being defensive, people react aggressively.

A quick note: It's possible to turn the dial up to "too courageous" in a toxic culture where speaking too courageously could lead you to face discipline or even lose your job. If that's the case, there are probably some underlying issues that need to be addressed in the area of belonging before you can work on creating healthier team habits around communication.

TUNING THE DIALS

Clarity is what we're optimizing in communication. The good news is that when you know clarity is what you're aiming for, you can use it as a guideline to determine which axis you need to pull or push to reach the Goldilocks zone of communication patterns that keep the team driving forward.

Tune your team's communication dials:

» Audit your team's communication levels. Where are you communicating too much or too little? What team habits could you add or subtract to bring the levels into the Goldilocks zone?

» Keep in mind that as your team improves the way they work with each other, you'll need to keep moving those dials. What was once too little information can become too much information as they develop other efficient habits and increase the shared context. Schedule a check-up every quarter or six months to reassess the team's communication patterns.

The art of powerful communication is being able to continuously update those dials and be flexible as they change.

Specify What Needs to Be Communicated Now

As you dial in the right levels of frequency, detail, focus, and courage in your conversations, you also need to think about what information needs to be communicated now, what can wait until later, and how you'll deal with updates as information changes.

One of the reasons communication becomes "all now, all the time" is that the person with the information needs to share it rather than that the team needs to hear it.

The person with the information wants to get it out of their brain because they're afraid they'll forget otherwise, and they want to move on to something else. This creates the impulse to interrupt in order to push that information out, but the unintended effect is that everyone has to be responsive in the now even if the issue could wait until some other point.

Here's what to do instead.

- Start by writing a draft to get it out of your brain.
- Convert it into a structured message with a subject line or topic.
- Give an indication of the time sensitivity of the item in the topic using agreed-upon shortcodes (which we'll discuss later in this chapter).
- Be clear about what type of action you're requesting, who needs to perform that action, what the outcome is, and when it needs to be done.

Of course, some jobs are set up largely to support people who need to get information out of their heads quickly and get on with their work. These "Now Catchers" can be executive assistants, receptionists, or real-time operations managers whose role is to be responsive to incoming information and put those pieces of information into the right places so that they can be dealt with by the rest of the team.

For our communication channels to remain high-signal and ready to receive the important updates, the rest of the chatter and information needs to find a home somewhere else.

How do you know what needs to be communicated now versus what can wait?

COMMUNICATED NOW

- Important priority shifts
- Progress updates that will alter your team's work over the next two to three days
- Additional resources that can be brought to bear to remove road-blocks or bottlenecks your team is facing
- Critical changes in capacity because a teammate is out or a capability you thought you had is no longer there

- Anything that falls under the communication requirements you wrote into your plan
- Critical updates or information shifts that may alter what people have prepared to discuss during a meeting (because it turns out that some souls like to actually prepare for a meeting)

COMMUNICATED LATER

- Anything that falls outside those categories can be communicated later, whether in a weekly update, a meeting, a project channel, or wherever else your team has decided such information should live

 **ROCKET PRACTICE**

COMMUNICATION CADENCES

Ask yourself these questions to build better team habits around when information gets communicated.

What is the right cadence of communication around this item, task, or project?

If you have a weekly or monthly update, is there information that gets stuffed into that update or meeting that may need to be at a different cadence? One way to find out is to notice how frequently someone asks for an update about information that's in the weekly or monthly meeting. If they're asking for it daily, you should probably be having a daily standup focused on that information.

On the flip side, pay attention to the information that shows up in daily or weekly reports and meetings that is never actually discussed or used. That can probably be elevated to a monthly format, or maybe it doesn't need to be in a meeting format. Instead, maybe it goes into a monthly team digest.

Who Really Needs to Know this Information, and Why?

When in doubt, defer to everyone knowing. As we'll talk about in the chapter on collaboration, making sure everyone has maximum visibility of all aspects of the work your team is doing is critical.

While you generally want to share information in a place where everyone can access it, be clear about calling out who needs to do something with this information. Otherwise, you end up with a broad update that everyone ends up setting aside in favor of their higher-priority work. (Remember, "somebody" never does anything.)

Do You Need to Have a Conversation about This Information or Just Confirm That It Was Read?

If you mainly want to know that people saw a piece of information, be clear that no response or action is needed aside from a thumbs-up. (Technologies such as Slack or Twist make this easy.) If a conversation does need to take place around the information, be clear about when and how that conversation will take place.

CRAFT CLEAR COMMUNICATION

Now that we've looked at the habits that make everyone's life easier when it comes to the broader cadence and flow of communication in your team, let's talk about how to craft pieces of communication so they're optimized for clarity. Good communication should be proactive, preemptive, and brief.

Proactive

Proactive means letting people know what's going on without being prompted for a status update. Don't make your teammate or manager come to you to ask how a project is going. Instead, put yourself in their shoes, anticipate when they'll become antsy for answers, and try to stay ahead of that moment.

Proactive communication is about taking the initiative and removing the emotional anxiety and burden of whoever feels the need to track down information that you have.

Preemptive

Preemptive communication is about thinking through the questions people might have about whatever you're communicating and trying to answer them before they need to be asked.

Take planning an event, for example. If I send you an email to say there's a team barbecue next week, you'll have some fairly predictable follow-up questions:

- When will it be?
- Where will it be?
- Is there a dress code?
- Are partners and families invited?
- Do I need to bring anything?

My goal in sending you an event invitation should be to think through what my guests will want to know in advance and preemptively answer those questions in the invitation. That prevents a couple of problems.

First, I won't have guests stressing about what to wear, whether they should eat ahead of time, or what time they're supposed to show up. Second, I will save myself a lot of work when seven people respond asking the same damn question.

More subtly, preemptive communication also increases belonging by making sure that everyone has the same level of context.

A few years ago, I was the emcee at an event. I told the host I planned to give the attendees a quick orientation to tell them where the food and bathrooms were and what the accessibility features were.

The host said, "Charlie, we didn't invite you here to tell people where the bathrooms are. They can figure it out."

My answer was that my job as the emcee was to make people feel comfortable, help them settle in, and answer their questions before they asked. I didn't have any ego about being the guy who told them where the bathrooms were.

Proactive, preemptive communication takes the emotional burden off the people you're communicating with. It might not seem like a big deal to know where the break-room facilities are, but what if you're a new mother who needs to run out and pump breast milk between speakers? It may not seem like a big deal to point out the food, but what if you rushed here from another meeting and know you can't pay full attention without a snack? Maybe only two people in that audience need to know about the accessibility features, but calling them out lets them know they belong here, just as everyone else does.

Preemptive communication ensures that everyone is operating from the same level of context, which puts people at ease and makes the space for them to bring their whole selves to work so they can participate more fully.

To return to the team barbecue example, if your team has been together for years, maybe you don't need to be explicit about the dress code. But if there is a new team member, they might not know your team's social norms. Will there be kosher or vegetarian options? Are children welcome? Does the event start promptly at 5 p.m., or is some cultural tardiness the norm?

Brief

I've just told you to preemptively, proactively answer every possible question a teammate might have when you send that project update. In an ideal world, you've *also* done this without being overly long.

In the dominant US business culture, brevity can be conflated with rudeness. We see longer communication as more human, more approachable—even more authentic. But in reality, adding a bunch of fluff to a communication that should be purely transactional is unkind to the recipient.

Most of us do genuinely care about how our teammates are doing—*and* we know they're drowning in a sea of communication, just as we are.

Being brief is an incredible kindness to your teammates. Brief, proactive, preemptive communications are easier to read, easier to decipher, easier to respond to, and therefore easier to clear from your inbox so you can get back to doing the real work.

It's entirely possible to communicate low-context information concisely, but it takes practice.

- **Use the Five-Sentences Rule.** Limit all email responses to five sentences or fewer. This forces you to think more concisely and stay more focused. As a bonus, shorter emails are easier to respond to, which means you're more likely to receive a reply.
- **Cut one-third.** Practice cutting one-third of the words you normally would use out of every communication.
- **Make it scannable.** When formatting a longer communication, use numbered lists, bullet points, and subheadings to make it as scannable as possible.
- **Use simpler versions of complex terms.** A lot of the verbose words that make us sound smart have one- or two-syllable equivalents that are easier to understand, faster to say, and more universally understood. For example, say "use" instead of "utilize."

If you're worried that your communications will come across as curt and rude, communicate that you're being brief to give yourself permission to do so.

Note: When it comes to belonging and bonding conversations, like asking how a teammate's weekend was or checking in to see if you can help them with a personal issue, you don't need to be brief. When you write an update letter to an old school friend, feel free to channel the flowery missives from the good old days of letter writing.

But when you're in transaction mode, err on the side of communicating succinctly.

ROCKET PRACTICE

REDUCE THE CHATTER

» Aim for a point where your single communiqué does all the lifting, and the most people have to do in response is give you a thumbs-up (or the equivalent). When you get that thumbs-up, you know you've proactively told them what they need to know without having to be asked and preemptively answered any questions they might have had. (Compare this to intent-based decisions in Chapter 4 on decision-making.)

» If you don't have all the details when you send a message, preempt questions by letting people know what's missing, when you expect to share it, and what channel to look for it in.

» Put yourself in the shoes of the person with the least shared information and common context: your new teammate, someone from a nondominant culture, etc. What information do they need to know?

» If previous communications or briefs exist, refer to them (and link to them if possible so that people don't have to look for them).

» Amplify the goal or intent of the event or action being communicated about so that we're on the same page not only about *what* needs to happen and *how* but also *why*.

USE SHORTCODES TO INCREASE COMMUNICATION SPEED AND CLARITY

One way to pack a lot of information into a few words is by using communication shortcodes. When incorporated into your team habits, shortcodes can help make your communications mercifully brief but still information-rich.

Of course, they can also make your communications overwhelming and indecipherable. When too many shortcodes are used without context, they can have an effect opposite to the clarity and time saving they're meant to provide.

Shortcodes require a high level of context to be effective. If I'm talking about financial reporting and say that our accountant has adhered to GAAP rules, then it's probably clear to the person I'm communicating with that I mean "generally accepted accounting principles." I've not only said a lot in a small amount of language, but I've also been much more specific than if I said our accountant followed regulations. Which regulations? What accounting principles?

However, if you're new to the team, we're not talking about finances, or you've never heard of GAAP, then I've made things more confusing. You and I don't have the high-level context required for me to throw around acronyms like GAAP.

You need to train new teammates in the shortcodes. At Productive Flourishing, we keep a codex of internal jargon that includes all the acronyms, shortcodes, and phrases that are unique to our organization. When we bring on a new teammate, we refer them to our team codex so they can get up to speed.

Here are some that we use at Productive Flourishing.

TASK/PROJECT TIMING

- **#U:** Urgent. This needs your attention in the next couple of hours. (Use sparingly.)
- **#EOD:** This needs your attention by the end of the day.
- **#ND:** This needs your attention by the end of the next day.
- **#EOW:** This needs your attention by the end of the week.
- **#NW:** This needs your attention sometime next week.
- **#TM:** This needs your attention this month.

(Note: When you specify a time frame, it's incredibly helpful to specify why it's necessary. I don't often tell my team something needs to be done by Thursday unless I really need it then, so if I specify that, they know it's a hard deadline. Otherwise, I would have said "this week," knowing that they're autonomous human beings who set their own priorities throughout the week.)

DECISION-MAKING

- **UYBJ:** Use your best judgment. "You have all the information you need to make a decision, and this is your call to make."
- **LMK:** Let me know. "Let me know whatever call you end up making."
- **DRIP:** Decision, recommendation, intention, or plan.
- **DRIP?:** Used when someone feels that another person's recommendation/intention requires more clear explanation.
- **DWWFY:** Do what works for you.
- **L1, L2, L3:** What level of decision this is. Level 1 = decide and don't tell me. Level 2 = decide and tell me. Level 3 = it's my decision, but please provide a DRIP. (These three levels of decision-making were discussed in Chapter 4.)

PLANNING

- **#Asana:** "Create a task in Asana and add relevant people as followers."
- **BOLO:** Be on (the) lookout. "Be ready to act, and watch for some event that might be a trigger action."
- **CQ:** Curious question. Used when I'm (Charlie) asking a question that could be read as critical but is legit neutral curiosity.
- **KISS:** Keep it simple, superstar.
- **NNTR:** No need to respond.

COMMUNICATION

- **BLUF:** Bottom line up front. Used to tell someone what's going on at the beginning of a communication rather than at the end (which they may not get to). Can be synonymous with a preemptive "TL;DR" (Too long; didn't read).
- **UIHO:** Unless I hear otherwise. Used to give a course of action that will be taken. A great shortcode for practicing intent-based communication.

- **UYHO:** Unless you hear otherwise. Used to set teammates on a course and not have them stall because of what might occur.
- **COPU:** Common operating picture update. More than just a heads-up, this shortcode lets teammates know that something important has shifted that they need to know about.

ROCKET PRACTICE

DEVELOP SHORTCODES

» Start a document with the shortcodes, abbreviations, and slang your team already uses, and write it clearly enough that an outsider can understand it. Could more shortcodes be added to your communications?

» How can you incorporate task and project timing shortcodes into your communications to ensure that everyone on the team quickly understands expectations and priorities?

BE INTENTIONAL AND CONSISTENT WITH COMMUNICATION MEDIUMS

We have an increasing number of ways to get in touch with our teammates. Video call, phone, email, Slack message, DM on social media, text message . . . if we're in an office, we could even stand up from our desk and walk across the room to talk to them in person.

The downside of this proliferation of communication mediums is—you guessed it—a lack of clarity. **Not only do we have to hunt through multiple places to find where a particular piece of information was sent, we also may not know how important a message is.**

Some mediums are by default higher priority than others. If you receive an email in the middle of the night, the sender probably couldn't sleep and decided to send you a note. If you receive a phone call, you'll answer with your heart pounding, wondering what's wrong.

As a team, do yourselves all the kindness of narrowing down the number of mediums you use to communicate and specifying which ones should be used for which messages.

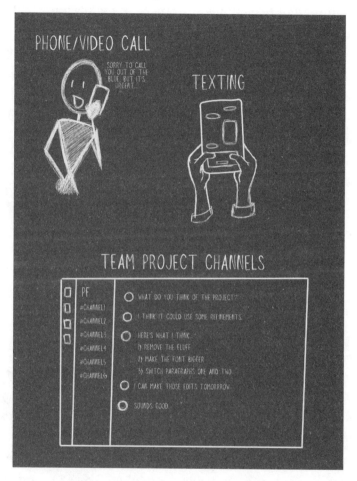

For example, at Team PF we use the following:

- Confluence: strategy and detail documents for reference
- Asana: project tasking and conversations about execution
- Google Docs: comments or questions about specific content
- Slack: in-the-moment questions and conversations (often with a link to the related project or content in Asana, Confluence, or Google Docs)

Phone or Video Call

Phone calls should be urgent—you need to receive or provide a piece of information right this minute. If you're calling a teammate out of the blue, you should have a good reason for it.

Keep in mind the principle of what needs to be communicated now versus later, and take advantage of asynchronous tools to do so with voice memos and videos. Some things can be much more easily and clearly explained verbally than by taking the time to write a long email, but instead of calling a teammate and interrupting their work, consider recording a Loom to talk through a message and then sending them a link in a less urgent channel.

Text

Text should be used only for time-sensitive transactional information.

There are times when you might text someone if an issue is not urgent—if you're on the road and don't have access to a computer and you need to send the information before you go off the grid for a long weekend, but it's not meant to be urgent.

Do your team a favor and specifically mention those reasons. As I've said, every request for information is a request for attention, and additional stress and anxiety are associated with certain channels. If you immediately call out that it's not urgent, everyone can disarm and chill.

In the cases where I need to do this, I might say, "Please move this to Confluence" or whatever channel it belongs in so that we don't continue the pattern of communicating about something that's not urgent on an urgent channel.

Team Project Channels

These should be used to communicate about project-specific issues that aren't urgent. You can set up project channels in Slack, Twist, Teams, Basecamp—whatever tool you use to coordinate your team.

Be careful of developing a team habit that treats messages in a group chat as urgent. As Jason Fried, the founder and CEO of 37Signals (makers of Basecamp), said on Twitter, "Group chat is like being in an all-day meeting, with no agenda, and random participants. It's the modern communications conveyor belt that never ends, divides your attention, fractures your time, and chains you to FOMO. It hurts work more than it helps."[2]

One good team habit to build into your team communication tool is using subject lines and threads to clearly indicate the topic and keep conversations together so team members don't have to jump around looking for information. They can simply scan subject lines, find the information, and get back to work.

 **ROCKET PRACTICE**

CREATE YOUR MEDIUM MAP

» As a team, decide which messages belong in the various mediums you use to communicate. How should the most urgent messages be sent? Which medium will you use for real-time collaboration? Do teammates have different individual preferences for certain mediums?

CHAPTER 7 TAKEAWAYS

- Tune your team's communication levels for clarity by dialing in your frequency, detail, focus, and courage.
- Understand what needs to be communicated now versus what can be communicated later. Build team habits to make sure communication channels stay clear so timely information can get through.
- Good communication should be proactive, preemptive, and brief.
- Use shortcodes to help keep your communications brief but still information-rich.
- As a team, narrow down the number of mediums you use and specify which ones should be used for which messages.

EIGHT COLLABORATION

> *None of us, including me, ever do great things.*
> *But we can all do small things, with great love,*
> *and together we can do something wonderful.*
>
> — MOTHER TERESA

There's a famous comedy skit by Abbott and Costello, "Who's on First?"[1] In the skit, Abbott tries to tell Costello the names of the players on a baseball team: "Who's on first, What's on second, I Don't Know's on third."

The confusion this causes — "Who's on first? How should I know?" — is hilarious because of how long it takes to resolve. It's less funny when you're at work and trying to resolve who's doing what work and the answer is "I don't know." (Third base!)

A well-defined team has a natural default answer to who's on first and what's on second. When a customer sends a question, a blog post needs to be written, or an expense needs approval, a team with good collaboration habits doesn't have to think twice about whose role it is.

Why are defaults so important? They reduce the number of small decisions and negotiations that happen throughout the workday — should you take that responsibility, or should I? Whose job description does this part of the project fall under?

The goal is to eliminate any confusion about who's in charge of which parts of the workflow so that all roles and responsibilities are extremely clear. All that extra energy we've been wasting asking "Who's on first?" can instead be funneled into pushing work forward in meaningful ways.

In the past few years, we've seen what happens when defaults vanish on a large scale. The big shift of COVID-19 took all our default patterns, all our team habits, all our workways and dumped them over the side of the boat. All the unspoken things had to be addressed because the structures and defaults of our days vanished overnight.

COVID-19 took the normal levels of collaboration negotiation we were dealing with day to day and multiplied them by orders of magnitude, given how human interactions scale. This increased cognitive load has contributed to the burnout we've been seeing over the past few years, and it's my hope that it has also illuminated the importance of defining intentional defaults that truly work for us.

Defining intentional team collaboration habits means looking at your team as a whole rather than focusing on the individuals. Most workers want to do a great job. Most are trained and competent; most want to show up and have great relationships with their teammates. If they're not doing that, something else is broken.

When we see a team that seems to be falling behind, our instinct is to figure out what's wrong with a specific person. But the far better approach is to ask, "What about the team's habits is at play that we can address that will benefit everyone and lighten the load for everyone—not just now but in the future?"

It's not that it's never an individual's behavioral problem. But, as a general rule, it's not the first place to look. If you start with the system and culture that the individual is working in, you won't find a simple problem that can be easily solved by fixing one person. Instead, start asking, what are the conditions that are leading to team members missing deadlines, duplicating work, and falling behind?

Let's start by looking at the composition of the team itself.

WHO'S ON YOUR TEAM?

Team composition is one of the first things I look at when I'm brought in as a workplace consultant and told a team isn't collaborating well. That's because when a team isn't collaborating well, it usually has less to do with the individuals involved and more to do with the fact that they're having to fight against the structure of their team composition.

Let's look at who should be on your team at a macrolevel, a micro-level, and a specialist level.

Is Your Team "in Shape"?

The last few decades have seen significant innovation and experimentation with "flat" organizations, "circular" organizations, sociocratic organizations, self-organized organizations, and so on. This is a reaction to the power dynamics inherently created and reinforced by the traditional models, enabled by changes in technology that allow communication and collaboration to be scaled differently than in the past.

A significant portion of my work these days is guiding teams to build more open team structures while still ensuring that the necessary *functions* typically performed by roles in the traditional pyramid are distributed effectively across the team.

Since these new governance models are unfamiliar to many people, it's easiest to start with the five levels of traditional organizations to show how the functions within teams work with each other:

- **Level 5**: Executives
- **Level 4**: Senior managers, master-level technical specialists, and advisors
- **Level 3**: Coordinators, junior managers, and advanced technical specialists
- **Level 2**: Specialists
- **Level 1**: Entry-level employees

Counting the number of team members at every level can give you a sense of whether an organization is "in shape." If you imagine a structure where every junior manager oversees four to eight level 1 and 2 people, every senior manager oversees four to five junior managers, and the executive (or small executive team) oversees the senior managers, a pyramid emerges. This is the typical structure of a healthy traditional organization.

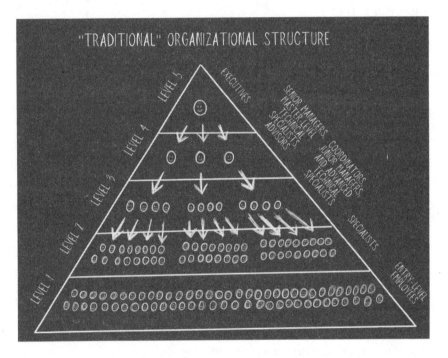

Teams and organizations that are "out of shape" come in a handful of varieties. There are hourglasses, which have a bunch of executives and visionaries at the top, a bunch of assistants or virtual assistants at the bottom, and no one in the middle to manage it all. There are diamonds, which are stuffed with managers who don't have anyone to give work to. There are upside-down pyramids, which have plenty of executives and managers, but no one at the bottom doing the work.

One client's small company had an organizational structure that was essentially an executive and two managers. This enabled me to predict all sorts of challenges with collaboration. Namely, with no one to do the

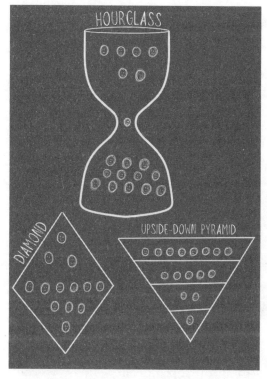

more entry-level and specialized work, the two people in the managerial positions essentially dropped to the entry-level specialist positions and the executive dropped to the managerial positions — which left no one at the top of the organization to do the planning, goal-setting, prioritizing, and envisioning work that the organization needed.

The team wasn't collaborating the way they should, but it had nothing to do with the teammates themselves. The team just didn't have the right composition. Hiring additional level 1 and level 2 employees helped bring the team back into shape.

Let's take a customer service function as another example of how understanding team structure can help you troubleshoot collaboration. If you start running into bottlenecks like poor call times or poor customer response times, you don't necessarily start by looking at the performance of the chief of customer happiness. You start with a simple question: "Do we have enough people responding to emails and answering phone calls?"

If the answer is no, hire more. If the answer is yes, work your way up the pyramid. Are they being managed well? Yes? Then there must be something about the foundations and structures and strategies that's making the setup not work.

Understanding the big picture of your team's overall shape can be a useful tool for troubleshooting collaboration. It can also be helpful to zoom in on the smallest unit of a team: the doer-reviewer-coordinator triad.

Doer-Reviewer-Coordinator Triad

Three roles make up the atomic elements of the team:

- **Doers** are the people rolling up their sleeves to make the work happen.
- **Reviewers** keep an eye on the quality of the output so the doers can stay focused on production. Reviewers can be editors, code reviewers, auditors, or proofreaders.
- **Coordinators** have two jobs: coordinating the doer and reviewer and coordinating with elements outside the team. A coordinator can be a manager, but it is often a communication role.

These roles might be shared and interchanged as the project requirements change, but knowing who the doer, reviewer, and coordinator are is useful for determining how you're going to collaborate and reducing the cognitive, emotional, and social load of a small team.

When I'm troubleshooting in an organization or team, I typically start with this triad (or these three essential functions). Do we have as many doers as we need to manage the workload? Are there enough reviewers to keep the work flowing without causing bottlenecks? Do we have someone (or a couple of someones) coordinating all this work?

If the team is bloated, I try to push them to define atomic team units within the larger group because smaller teams tend to be much faster than bigger ones. A two-person doer-reviewer team can sync really well. They have a strong sense of their roles and can communicate clearly about workflow so it doesn't become a logistical and managerial burden for the reviewer or create many backlogs for the doer. Then, the communicator can coordinate between them and communicate adequately with others on the larger team.

Thinking about teams in terms of the doer-reviewer-coordinator triad allows you to build the smallest possible atomic team to make something happen. It also gives you a functional way to intuit where to add to the team without taking a shot in the dark. If your doer is cranking faster than your reviewer can keep up, you need more reviewers. If your doer-reviewer dyad is creating more units of work than are being adequately sent to other teams, you need to increase your coordinator capacity.

 FRAMEWORK

TIMWOOD

TIMWOOD (transportation, inventory, motion, wait time, overproduction, overprocessing, and defects) is a framework that comes from the lean space to help identify the common sources of waste in a team or organization.

In most creative businesses, we should be watching out for motion, waiting, overprocessing, and defects.

Motion: If your team is actively trying to get work done but not actually accomplishing anything, that excess motion could be a result of a lack of clarity, constantly shifting goals and priorities, or too many handoffs when fewer people or steps would be better.

Wait Time: Is the doer waiting for assignments from the coordinator or comments from the reviewer? Is the reviewer waiting for work from the doer? Where can the process be accelerated, or who can be added to the team to increase capacity?

Overprocessing: Unnecessary mini–review cycles and constant tweaking of work that just needs to ship can hold up projects without actually increasing quality.

Defects: Someone spends three days trying to nail a piece of website copy, but when they turn it in, it's just not where it needs to be, causing the whole team to scramble to keep the project on track.

TIMWOOD is a great tool to diagnose what's happening in terms of the collaboration in your team and where you can eliminate waste.

Know Which Wolf to Call

In the Quentin Tarantino film *Pulp Fiction*, hitmen Vincent and Jules are faced with an unfortunate incident involving Marvin in the back seat of their car. They're in a jam, and they need someone to get them out of it fast. They make a call, and a few minutes later, a door opens to reveal Harvey Keitel standing on the doorstep in a tuxedo at 8:45 a.m. "I'm Winston Wolf," he says by way of introduction. "I solve problems."

Every team needs a Mr. Wolf or five on hand to handle the problems that pop up. Who's your grammar guru? Your website wizard? Your spreadsheet whisperer, your technical savant, your customer happiness rock star? That's the person you call when you have a specialized problem.

Everyone on the team should be the Wolf of something, whether they're a senior member with long-standing experience or a junior member with an uncanny ability to read people.

Think of an auto shop. Most mechanics can perform a wide range of services on a wide range of vehicles. But in every shop, you'll find a few Wolfs—the person you call when that exotic import comes in or when you can't chase down a gremlin in the electronics system. They're the ones with an encyclopedic knowledge of esoteric subjects, and when you've tried everything else, you can call Julie and she'll just *know* that there's a faulty wire in that year's batch of Corvette C3 Fastbacks.

But just because someone is the default—the Wolf—doesn't mean that they can or should be the only person who can do a certain job. That creates a bottleneck, especially if the particular problem they solve comes up regularly. What happens if they're out of the office or busy with another project? Because of this, ideally, there's some knowledge transfer when a Wolf comes in to solve a problem. When your spreadsheet whisperer comes in to help another team member set up a VLOOKUP function, they should also be teaching their teammate to do it on their own next time.

If it's a scenario that happens once or twice a year, though, it might make the most sense to have one person be the Wolf. It's not reasonable to expect everyone on the team to have Julie's knowledge of Corvette electronics. It's usually better to build team mastery of more commonly used high-value skills and leave the rare skills to the Wolfs.

How do people become Wolfs? Over time, members of a team that has a degree of autonomy and choice will start to self-select what they want to be subject matter experts in. This should absolutely be encouraged. If someone self-selects to be the Wolf of a thing, it's likely because they're curious and motivated by that thing—even if that task seems like drudgery to other members of the team. The Wolf will typically be excited to be tagged, and problems will be solved faster.

ROCKET PRACTICE

TROUBLESHOOT TEAM COMPOSITION

» Look at your team's shape. Where might collaboration be improved by shifting roles and responsibilities?

» Who are the default doers, reviewers, and coordinators on your team? Do you have enough of the right people in the right places? If not, who can shift within the current team to create a good workflow?

» Who is the Wolf for different critical functions on your team? Are there any gaps where you need a Wolf but don't have a clear person to call? If so, who knows that, and how has it been communicated?

» Is there room in the work you do together for teammates who currently aren't the Wolf of anything to begin developing specialties? How do you as a team support them in becoming a Wolf so that they have a greater sense of belonging on the team and you have fewer gaps in the team itself?

OPEN THE BLACK BOX

Now that we've explored the question of *who* your team defaults are, let's talk about defaults around *how* work gets done. Unfortunately, in many teams, the answer is "I don't know." (Third base!)

In computing, a black box is a system where you can see the inputs and outputs but have no idea what the internal workings are. It's like a top-secret factory where widgets go in and bicycles come out, but you have no idea what happened inside to get from widget to bicycle.

Black boxes happen in teams all the time. You may know your teammate is doing great work because you see the final product, but you have no idea how they do it or what they're working on at any given moment.

The challenge of a black box is that if I don't know what a teammate is working on in the moment, I might start to initiate the same work. Or I may start becoming anxious about whether the work is happening at all and whether I need to check in or start worrying that I'll have to jump in at the last minute. This can also create trust issues. If I can't see the work you're doing and decide to do it myself to be on the safe side, I've implicitly shown that I didn't trust you to do the work yourself.

It's time to open the black boxes of where work happens and how it is assigned.

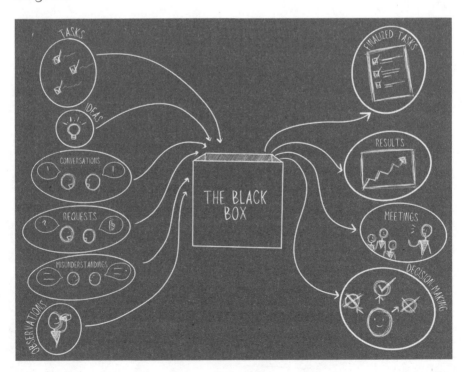

Where Does Work Happen?

There's a long-standing preoccupation in our working environments with seeing people work in real time. The idea seems to be that if you can't see what your people are doing, they could be doing anything. Translated to the knowledge workplace, this looks like open-office floor plans, in-person work requirements, and even software that tracks a remote employee's computer.

If our goal is to hire people to do their best work, this preoccupation with watching them work creates a mismatch. I might do my best work offline in a coffee shop, where no one can keep tabs on me. If I were working on a team that needed me to sit in a specific location so the manager could visually check what I was doing, I would be highly incentivized not to do my highest-value work but instead to do work that I could accomplish in the place where people want to see me work.

We all work in our own unique ways, using our own different tools. Unless you're collocated and looking at someone else's screen, you don't really know what they're working on at any given moment. But you can develop team habits that allow people to do their highest-value work in the way that works for them while providing visibility and accountability so that they can collaborate well with their teammates.

The way to do this is to decide on default tools and channels that you use as a team and make sure all team work happens in those places. (See the last chapter for more.)

The power of having default tools such as Google Docs or Dropbox or places where you can work collaboratively is that you can easily see what people are working on while allowing them to work in the way that's most productive for them. It answers both questions of where do we do our best work as individuals and where is the default place we collectively work as a team.

How Do Check-Ins Happen?

In order to collaborate well, we need to be aware of what other team members are working on. Yet asking questions like "What did you do today?" or "Where are we on this project?" can immediately make people defensive.

Ideally, you don't have to ask those questions because your team has already worked on the habit of proactive, preemptive communication that we discussed in the previous chapter. But when you do need to ask, make it clear that you're being positive rather than grilling them for information. Here's where an emoji can go a long way (unless you have a team habit of using emojis passive aggressively). Professors Tomoko Yokoi and Jennifer Jordan of the International Institute for Management Development (IMD) have been studying effective leadership in the digital age and argue that using emojis can be a powerful way to connect with teammates.

As they write in *Harvard Business Review*, "Employees don't check their emotions at the office door—or Zoom room."[2] Emojis can help us enhance our communication when we're not together face-to-face.

"What did you get into today? 🎨 🛹 💪 " conveys more emotional context than "What did you get into today?" without emojis and can serve as an alternative to the physical cues that many teams and leaders use to convey that context in person.

How Is Work Assigned?

Along with black boxes around where the work is done, you can also have black boxes around how teammates are tasked. A lot of teams develop a haphazard "choose your own" way of giving someone else a task. The problem is if you have five different channels where you can give someone a task and six people on your team, for any given person, there are at least twenty-five different configurations of how they might receive tasks from another teammate.

For example, Alex texts you about a project because that's their preferred method of communication. You relay one task to Suanna via email and then hop on Slack to DM Hallie about her part of the project. Since Alex has no visibility of your email or Slack DMs, they might start wondering what work was assigned. Hallie and Suanna might start duplicating work, not knowing that you also talked to the other person, or they might hop on a quick video call together to discuss the project and come up with a ghost plan (see Chapter 6) without looping in you and Alex.

Eliminating black boxes reduces the overprocessing and duplication of work that happens when we aren't sure what our teammates are working on. It also reduces wait times because we don't have to check in for progress reports, which might hold up our own work. And, of course, it cuts down on those inevitable Crisco watermelons that happen when the time comes to hand off work.

How Are Tasks Described?

Along with being clear about where work is done and how tasks are assigned, be clear about what the task is. As a rule of thumb, when you write a task list, write it as if some other person in the future will have to read it and act with no further explanation.

If I'm in our team's Asana workspace and see an incoherent task—especially one that's overdue—I can't do anything to help with it. I don't know what "Email list" means without tracking down whoever wrote the task. Cull the email list? Send an email to the list? Research new mailing list providers?

Incoherent tasks introduce extra wait time into the collaborative process. They also limit your teammates' ability to help. In Chapter 5, we talked about how amazing the force multipliers in the group can be. If you've written a well-structured task in the place where your team does work, it's easier for that force multiplier to step in and help out. It's easier for you to take a break if needed, to step off the grid for a long weekend and come back to find that the entire team's work didn't stall because you left those bread crumbs to show where the work was and what else needed to happen.

Always write your tasks and thread topics as if some other person will need to read them, because that other person might be *you* in the future when you are sidetracked from a project for a few weeks, only to come back to a mystifying, out-of-context set of notes that you left for yourself.

Writing clear task descriptions takes care of yourself in the future and takes care of your teammates in the now and in the future.

What Is Your Team's Project Pace?

When your team is collaborating well, you end up with a natural cadence for how long the project is, how much you are updating, how fast it's moving along, and so forth. If that cadence doesn't seem to be in sync with the real timeline of the project, it's a solid indicator that your collaboration may not be as tight as you think it is or as tight as it needs to be.

For example, if you have a project deadline at the end of the quarter, you can look at the pace of how far you've advanced at the end of the first month and reevaluate the ways in which your team is collaborating to meet that timeline. Are you on target to hit the end-of-quarter deadline at your current pace of one work session per week? Or do you need to increase the pace of work sessions in order to complete the project on time?

Be aware that your project pace could also point to other factors such as capacity, resources, or how realistic the plan or goal was to begin with. If your collaboration seems to be on point, start digging into these other factors.

TEAMWORK IN TEAM CHANNELS

Opening the black boxes around where work happens and how work is assigned helps reduce the cognitive overload, emotional anxiety, and general stress associated with a team's collaboration efforts.

» Where does work happen by default? Why there? Does this work for us? Does it give us the Goldilocks amount of visibility of what our teammates are doing so we can honor their work and not inadvertently duplicate or negate it?

» What are our team defaults for proactively sharing what we're working on and for checking in when we need to know the status of a project?

» What are the default channels that we use to have conversations about projects or to task our coworkers? Are those channels giving our teammates the right amount of visibility of other parts of the project? Is it simple to scan back through and find information in that channel?

» What are our team conventions for writing task titles and descriptions? Are we using verbs to make it clear what action is needed? Are we leaving clear enough bread crumbs for our teammates to understand what the task requires of them? Have we provided enough information for our teammates to get straight to work instead of wasting time hunting down more details?

» If our project pace is off, do we need more doers on the project to speed up the pace? Do we have enough reviewers to keep the work that's being created from being bottlenecked? Are we having trouble at the coordinator level because the work that's been finished is not being passed efficiently between team members or outside the team? Is there any TIMWOOD waste we can cut to accelerate the process?

CREATE THE TEAM HABIT OF FORMING AD HOC PROJECT TEAMS

For my whole life, when I've seen a problem, my natural tendency has been to look around and see who's there to help me solve it. It's a by-product of growing up in a military family and spending my formative years in the Boy Scouts and the Army.

Because I grew up this way, I assumed ad hoc team building was a natural tendency for everyone: See a problem, look around the table, form a team to stand up and solve the problem, and then disband.

As I've learned, this isn't a natural and fluid impulse for many people. Yet it can be an extremely powerful skill to cultivate.

When you teach communities how to create community response teams, it empowers them to be more self-sufficient and develop the capabilities to solve big and small problems. **When you teach people within** an organization to stand up temporary teams to solve problems and pursue opportunities, they unlock a valuable skill.

One of the questions I started asking as a workplace consultant is "Who gets to charter a team?" The answer often is that the workplace has unnecessary structures and defaults that make it hard for people to form a dynamic team to solve a particular problem.

Sometimes people don't form teams because they're sensitive to adding work for their teammates. They know that everyone's probably working at capacity, just as they are, and don't want to put more work on anyone's plate.

Or they don't feel that they have permission—which is funny because if you ask an executive for permission to get together to fix a problem, they will be stupefied. Of course you can fix a problem! But maybe your team's culture prevents that by implicitly discouraging people to take the initiative. Standing up a team to solve a problem and failing puts you on the hook in a different way than if you stayed quiet about the problem.

One of the final barriers is the question "Who gets to lead?" When you start talking about a project leader or project manager, it creates a scenario where people who are not in a typical manager or leader role either don't think they're qualified to push that project forward, or their teammates default to someone else. It also unintentionally makes managers and leaders manage projects more than they need to, when what you really need is for someone to own a project and push it forward using the team that they have available.

A more useful way to think of managing teams is to ask the following question:

Who Owns the Project?

In the doer-reviewer-coordinator triad, the coordinator often ends up being the project owner. It doesn't have to be that way. The doer can be the project owner and be the person who is largely responsible for making it happen. Or the reviewer could own the project, driving both the doer and the coordinator.

Calling out the project owner is another way of being clear about who's on first. It tells the team who to reach out to if they have questions, who to report to when they've made progress on their part of the project, and who to celebrate for taking the initiative.

When someone has been designated the project owner (or takes on that role for themselves), they don't necessarily need to have the entire skill set to push a project through. They're responsible for assembling their team of Wolfs, keeping them on track, and reporting on project outcomes. They also gain the functional authority to tell someone who's higher up in the organizational chain to do something on a certain timeline to support that project.

When you create the team habit of assigning project owners, it allows more people to manage or lead projects, regardless of their rank and status within the organization. This has the wonderful benefit of increasing bench strength for product management and leadership across the organization.

It's an intuitive concept, *and* it intentionally blurs some of those level 1 through level 5 lines on the organizational pyramid.

The other upshot is that when you've been the project owner a few times, you become hyperkeen to be a good teammate in the future. You learn how to communicate and collaborate better on projects you don't own because you've been on the other side.

ROCKET PRACTICE

HOW TO STAND UP A TEAM

As a team, manager, or leader, ask the following questions: Who gets to create a team? How can we ensure that they have the support they need? In what ways are we disincentivizing people to stand up ad hoc teams to solve problems or pursue opportunities?

As an individual contributor who has spotted a problem and wants to stand up an ad hoc team:

» Don't assume that you have to be the sole person to fix it. Instead, consider yourself the project owner. You don't have to know how to do everything; you just need to know which Wolfs to call on to make it happen.

» Make your intentions clear. Say, "Hey, I see this particular issue or challenge. Unless I hear otherwise, I'm going to talk to a few folks and get together and solve it." In that case, you're not really asking for permission; you're just making sure you're not running with scissors and getting yourself and your teammates in trouble.

» Know that solving a long-standing problem or challenge may take longer than you expect. Many of the easy problems in organizations have already been solved. You may be trying to get rid of a simple broken printer, but you may also uncover a pernicious, entrenched problem.

» Pick a communication cadence and stick with it until you realize it's too much or too little. If it becomes a quarter-sized or longer project, apply the methodology in Part 3 on how to change a team habit.

CHAPTER 8 TAKEAWAYS

- A well-defined team has a natural default answer to whose job it is to perform any task that might arise.
- The atomic element of the team is the doer-reviewer-coordinator triad. Knowing who is in those roles allows you to troubleshoot the makeup of your team.
- Define which Wolf to call for any given problem that regularly comes up in your team.
- Team work (and conversations about that work) should be done in team channels.
- Any team member should have the ability to form an ad hoc project team to solve a problem.

NINE

MEETINGS

*In a good meeting, there is a momentum that comes
from the spontaneous exchange of fresh ideas
and produces extraordinary results.*

—HAROLD GENEEN

One of the reasons meetings are such a go-to for people when they're thinking of team habits to change is that they are the context in which all other team habits come into play.

You experience belonging and trust in real time. You see decision-making, goal-setting, and planning in action. Communication and collaboration habits pop up as you start talking about how you will work together to get it all done.

Meetings are one of those places where, in the span of an hour, you see all your bad team habits one after another in rapid succession. People talk over each other. People feel excluded from the process. The plan goes wonky (or it becomes clear that it was never there to begin with). Decisions are rushed, and next steps are lost. It's not clear who's on first, so "somebody" gets a lot of jobs.

Meetings are also painful because when we're in the middle of one—particularly one that's going badly—we're hyperaware that there's a bunch of other work we could be doing. Work that (hopefully) we find meaningful, challenging, and fulfilling. Work that (probably) someone else is going to call us out for not doing because we were stuck in this meeting.

It's a rare organization or team that can honestly say they love every meeting they have.

Meetings can be either a powerful force multiplier or a powerful force diminisher. Getting people together for a great meeting can create a leverage factor for a team's energy that can make something completely diffcrent and better. Or it can diminish your team's attention and capacity and keep them from doing the work they should be doing.

The great thing about focusing on meetings is that you don't need to go to senior executives for buy-in to improve them. You don't need to coordinate with another team or business unit to make changes. You can simply decide with your team that you're going to change your meeting culture into something that supports you in doing your best work.

All of this is why meetings are a great place to start when addressing team habits. But if you're still not convinced of the true cost of poorly done meetings, it's time to break out the calculator.

MEETING MATH

When the $500 office printer breaks, we have to fill out a requisition form or purchase order to replace it. That $500 gets scrutinized before it is approved—or not. But when we want to call a meeting? Nothing stops us, even though most meetings cost far more than $500 from the perspective of salaries and blocks of time.

In business, it is harder to get access to money, even though it is easier to get more of it, than it is to get access to the thing we have a massive shortage of: people's full engagement and attention.

Let's look at the true cost of a meeting.

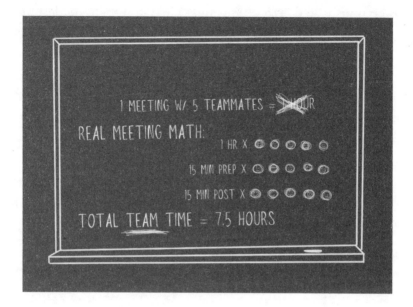

How Long Are Meetings, Actually?

You've called a one-hour meeting. How much time does that really soak up?

- Before the meeting: fifteen minutes of prep and transition. This is the time spent transitioning from whatever you were doing into meeting mode.
- Meeting time: the one hour of time *actually* scheduled for the meeting.
- After the meeting: fifteen to twenty minutes of exit and admin time. Most meetings create more work, whether that is sending out a message, spending time making a decision about what was discussed, or just transitioning back into deeper work.
- When you look at it this way, a one-hour meeting really takes up at least ninety minutes of your time.

How Many Meetings Do You Actually Have per Week?

You may look at your calendar and say you have between three and five standing meetings every week. Not bad, right? Until you start factoring in all the unexpected "crutch meetings" that pop up at the last minute. (Crutch meetings are meetings that act as a stand-in for a poor team habit; we'll talk about them in more detail in a minute.)

Normally when I do this exercise with clients, they'll tell me that 50 percent of the meetings they had last week were one-off meetings that don't normally happen. But when we go further back through their schedules, it becomes clear that "one-off" meetings essentially take up the same amount of time each week. They might as well be considered standing meetings, which means you need to take them into account in your schedule. (And then, as we'll discuss, figure out how to eliminate them.)

Taking crutch meetings into account, you may *actually* have eight standing meetings a week that average forty-five minutes each. Using the rule of thumb that there will be at least thirty minutes of prep and admin time before and after each meeting, that's a full ten hours of every workweek eaten up by meetings.

That leaves you thirty hours in a typical workweek to do the work you're ostensibly being paid to do. Not too bad, right?

Hold on just one second—it gets worse.

When Are Meetings Held?

When the meeting is held is just as important as how long it is. If you schedule a meeting at 8 a.m., for example, you catch most people in their warm-up cycle. Most people aren't ready for deep conversation at that time, which means the meeting will be longer than needed, more confusing than anticipated, or just plain useless.

What's more likely is that you put invisible work on your team to show up earlier to work to prepare for the meeting. Time spent preparing for the 8 a.m. meeting displaces the time your teammates were probably spending on self-care, family, or sleep.

Scheduling meetings at 9:30 or 10 a.m. isn't much better, but for different reasons. That midmorning meeting essentially ensures that your teammates don't get a full focus block on either side of the meeting. Unless they get to work super early, they will probably spend the morning on admin and then spend the hour after the meeting pushing things around before lunch. That hour-long meeting ends up demolishing an entire morning's worth of focused work.

At Team PF, we tend to schedule meetings at 11 a.m., 1 p.m., or 3 p.m. An 11 a.m. meeting gives people a good focus block of work in the morning, after which they can come to the meeting warmed up and ready. A 1 p.m. meeting harnesses that "just back from lunch" energy while leaving a solid amount of time in the afternoon for focus blocks, and 3 p.m. can be a powerful meeting time or not, depending on your team's chronotypes (which we will talk about more in the team core habits chapter).

This can be more difficult to manage with teams that span multiple time zones. The important thing is to work with your teammates to find the option that best fits all of your schedules.

The day on which meetings happen during the week can also be a force multiplier or diminisher because it determines the shape and cadence of the week. This is why we see so many planning and coordination meetings on Monday or Tuesday. If you schedule a planning meeting on Thursday, people are either frazzled or distracted by looming end-of-week deadlines. Whatever you planned during that meeting will be tough to remember by the following week.

It's less palpable, but the timing of certain types of meetings during a month can also shape the workflow of a month or quarter.

In our imaginary meeting math example, we've established that you technically have eight seventy-five-minute meetings throughout the week. Take a look at when they fall. How many of them are effectively torpedoing an entire morning's or afternoon's worth of work?

How Many People Are at the Meeting?

The final calculation in meeting math is this: If you have one hour-long meeting with eight people, *you're actually having twelve hours' worth of meetings*. (This is after we take into account the buffer time on either side of the meeting.)

You're using up eight hours of time and attention. Eight hours of people's salary. When you think about it that way, eliminating one meeting can eliminate that claim on eight people's attention and free up much more time for actual work to happen.

Meeting math is the answer to the question of why your team is having such a hard time pushing projects forward. Why are they not getting strategic work done? Why are they burning out? Why do they keep getting blocked by the strategic-recurring-urgent work logjams that we talked about in the chapter on planning?

Once you factor in meeting math, you can see why there's just not enough time in most people's calendars to do their work.

If they *are* getting work done, odds are that they're doing it in such a way that it is pushing them along the road to burnout because the only times they can find focus blocks are nights and weekends, when their schedule isn't being interrupted by meetings.

MEETING MATH EXAMPLE

Standing meetings per week	8 meetings
x Time spent per meeting (including buffer time)	1.5 hours
= Total time (per person) spent in meetings	12 hours
x Number of teammates	8 people
= Total team time spent in meetings	96 hours
x Average hourly pay	$50 per hour
= Amount spent on meetings per week	$4,800 per week

The team in the above example is spending $240,000 per year on meetings, yet no one can get approval to replace the printer that's been out-of-date for years.

I'm not trying to say that all meetings are bad. I *am* saying that I want your team to have meetings that intentionally and habitually act as a multiplying force of your team's ability to do their best work. Understanding meeting math can give you a powerful tool and language to start tackling team habits around meetings.

Eliminate Crutch Meetings

One question I often get asked is this: When counting meetings, should you note every quick one-on-one conversation with a teammate? What if you and a coworker ran by a third teammate's desk to straighten out your questions with a ten-minute chat? How many people need to be at a meeting for it to "count"?

When auditing your meetings, resist the urge to be legalistic about how to specifically define a meeting and instead go with the old mantra "I'll know it when I see it."

A quick meeting with a coworker can be a huge time saver. If you were gone for a couple of days, you could easily log in to Slack on your first morning back and spend ninety minutes sifting through threads to catch up. Or you could phone a friend and get caught up in five minutes. Was that technically a meeting? Don't worry about it too much.

You *do* need to be on the sharp lookout for when meetings become crutches for bad team habits in other categories.

Crutch meetings are used to address things that should be taken care of outside the meeting but aren't. Your plan keeps going off the rails, so you call a meeting to fix it. Your communication has broken down, so you call a meeting to get everyone on the same page. No one knows what the priorities are, so—you get the idea.

When you take a deeper look at people's overloaded meeting schedules, it becomes clear that many of those one-off meetings are actually crutch meetings. If you want to remove them from your schedule for good, you need to address what's causing them and get ahead of it.

The daily standup, which we touched on in the chapter on planning, is a good example of a potential crutch meeting. If you need to have a daily standup because you don't have another clear way to keep everyone on track, it's an expensive way to fix a planning problem. But it could also be the case that you're in a VUCA environment—such as a merger, reorg, or global pandemic—and the daily standup is the best way to quickly identify the day's priorities and update team members on new information.

What's Your Meeting Promoter Score?

Your meeting promoter score is a play on the net promoter score, which was created by Fred Reichheld and outlined in his book *The Ultimate Question*.[1] In the same way that marketers can get a quick sense of how well their product or company is doing based on the question "How likely are you to recommend [X] to a friend?," you can quickly discover whether a meeting was worthwhile by asking, "Would you recommend this meeting to a coworker?"

Meetings affect every one of us uniquely. If you're a social person, even mediocre meetings might be the highlight of your day. If you're an introvert, even showing up to the best meeting ever could be an energy drain.

As you explore team habit shifts around meetings, keep in mind that however you feel about meetings, others on your team might not feel the same way. **For a lot of people, having a meeting on the schedule adds an additional layer of anxiety to the day.**

Even a virtual meeting means having to put makeup on, having to be approachable, remembering to smile, or making small talk. There might be stressful logistical questions to answer, such as "Do I need to be on camera? Will the dogs start barking? What if I have to breastfeed? Do I need to tidy up my office?"

I could get on a call and talk all day, but that's not the case with most of my teammates. I know that every time I call a meeting, each of them has an additional level of negotiation that I am not necessarily privy to in order to show up for the meeting. I'm serious about that responsibility.

One of the things that surprises a lot of people when they join Team PF is that they tend to end meetings feeling glad that they were there. They leave more connected, inspired, and excited than they were before the meeting. We work hard to make sure that every meeting on the calendar is multiplying the force of our team's efforts rather than draining them.

AUDIT YOUR MEETINGS

» Look at your schedule of standing meetings on a weekly and monthly basis and then work through the meeting math above. To your best estimate, how much time and salary are being spent on meetings each week?

» When do meetings happen during the day? Do they impede potential focus blocks for your teammates? Is there a different time of day that would make more sense to ensure that everyone in attendance can engage? Be sure to account for teammates in different time zones.

» Does your weekly, monthly, and quarterly meeting schedule drive work forward and create force multiplication? Or does it diminish and squander the team's time, energy, and attention?

» How many meetings on your schedule in the last six weeks were actually crutch meetings? What faulty habit created the need for that meeting? Once you notice a trend, that's probably the next team habit to start working on.

» To determine whether a meeting is worth keeping on the schedule, ask yourself and your team, "Are you glad we had this meeting? Did it drive our energy and focus or disperse it? If you had to review it on Yelp, would you recommend it to a friend or teammate?" If the answer is no, the next question you need to ask is "What can we do to make our meetings less stressful, more effective, and more of an amazing force multiplier for the rest of our team?"

BUILDING BETTER MEETINGS

How many times have you walked into a conference room or logged in to Zoom with no clear idea of what the meeting you're about to attend is for?

Building better meetings starts with understanding that not all meetings are cut from the same cloth. **Every meeting falls into one of six categories, or is made up of blocks of those categories—many of which mirror the categories of team habits we've been talking about.**

When you start a team habit of defining meeting categories, it helps you put into perspective what meetings are necessary for what reasons. And, hopefully, relieves your teammates of the frustration of stepping into a conference room or logging on to a Zoom call without a clue as to what's going on.

The Six Meeting Blocks

Decision-Making Meeting

The point of a decision-making meeting is to get the appropriate number of people at the table to go from information to decision. Decision-making meetings are called either early in the process, when you know a decision is going to come up, or later on, when you have gotten stuck and need a decision to drive work forward.

Planning Meeting

Planning meetings are designed to get the team on board with a certain course of action and align your activity with a timeline. In an ideal world, most of the preliminary decisions would have been made before going into a planning meeting, but some planning meetings are designed to help inform the decisions that need to be made in order to execute the plan. Once you've had your planning meeting, you can then have a shorter decision-making meeting that includes just the required people.

Brainstorming Session

The goal of a brainstorming session is to generate potential solutions and courses of action. For a brainstorming session, the goal should be to keep expanding possibilities rather than distilling those ideas and options into actionable solutions.

Bonding Meeting

The main point of a bonding meeting is to build belonging and rapport by getting to know each other better. The topic of conversation should be work only insofar as it makes people more comfortable socializing.

I want to slow down on that point for a moment. A lot of facilitators tend to be extroverted quick thinkers and don't see the problem with ambushing teammates with a bunch of thoughtful icebreakers designed to get conversation flowing. But a lot of people would rather not just show up and talk about themselves without being given time to prepare. Having work-related conversations invites them into the conversation, as opposed to putting them on the spot with questions that can seem intrusive, like "What are your dreams?" or even "What are your plans for this weekend?"

We talked about one of my favorite questions for these types of meetings in the chapter on belonging: "What are your nonwork wins?" In my experience, anyone can engage with that question without feeling as if they are participating in some sort of public journaling exercise.

Review Meeting

The point of the review meeting (or debrief, or after-action review) is to look over a previous activity and see what worked and what didn't work and to develop insights that you can apply to current or future plans and projects.

Update Meeting

The job of the update meeting is to keep people informed about what's going on, distill the key information, and provide a place for people to ask questions. An update meeting is a sense-making meeting where you just help people make sense of what's happening around them.

I hesitated to put update meetings on this list because I've been to far too many update meetings that could have been an email or that were so packed with such high-level communication that I left feeling less clear about what was going on then when I went in.

A good rule of thumb for update meetings is that people should leave feeling more clear, aligned, and engaged with the work ahead. "Engaged" doesn't necessarily mean inspired and excited; resolute will do.

Using Meeting Blocks

Think of the six types of meetings as building blocks. You can choose from the blocks to create a meeting that builds belonging, helps you brainstorms ideas, and leads to decisions. Or you can create a meeting that provides updates on progress, then helps you decide on a path forward.

Thinking of each of these as separate blocks will improve your meetings in a few ways.

Build Complementary Meetings

Not all meeting blocks play well with one another. For example, having a bonding block after a review block can be difficult. If you are brutally honest about what went well and what went wrong during the review meeting, people might feel too defensive for a bonding exercise. There are ways of debriefing that build belonging, but it's tricky. As a facilitator, you need to know you're potentially playing with fire when you combine these two blocks.

While brainstorming, decision-making, and planning meeting blocks seem as if they naturally complement each other, they can also be problematic when included in the same meeting. Switching between those three mental states can be tough, which means that as a facilitator, you need to be very clear about what state you're in.

Call Out Block Switches

When a meeting slides from one type to another without the facilitator calling out that there has been a switch, it can feel confusing. People aren't sure how to engage, and they might not be sure what you need from them. Calling out what type of block you're in during a meeting lets your teammates know how to partner with you better at every step.

Let's go back to the example of brainstorming and decision-making. When used in the same meeting, they can either become a muddy mess or be extremely effective, depending on how well the facilitator calls out what phase the meeting is currently in. I recommend starting with brainstorming. Once the brainstorming session is over, make it clear that you are now in the deciding portion of the meeting. This gives everyone—especially the creative folks—the cue that it's not time for eighteen more ideas; it's time to pare the ideas down to the best ones.

Sometimes, meetings can make an unplanned shift into a different block. Update meetings in particular have a habit of sliding into decision-making, reviewing, and brainstorming. You will be on your third update point of seven when somebody jumps in to ask strategy questions or start brainstorming solutions. As a facilitator, it's your job to say, "I appreciate that, but the point of this meeting is to update. We'll schedule a separate conversation for brainstorming or planning."

Avoid Overstuffed Meetings

As you learn how your team works, you'll also develop a sense of how quickly you can get through topics and types of meeting blocks. If I see an agenda that has us brainstorming six topics in one hour, I know we will never get through it. Our team takes twenty minutes on average to get through a brainstorming block, which means we either need to reschedule the meeting to a longer time block, break it into parts, or find another way to do the brainstorming.

When looking at an overstuffed meeting, resist the urge to squeeze out the bonding block at the beginning or skip noting the next steps at the end. Both of those are hugely important parts of the meeting, and the five to ten minutes you'll save by cutting them will create downstream problems in team performance, belonging, and collaboration.

If you do need to squeeze something out of an agenda, do the hard work of triaging what needs to go into this meeting and deciding how you can get through the rest of the work elsewhere. And if you need multiple meetings to cover it all, then schedule multiple meetings. Don't try to crush everything into too short a time.

Set Clear Agendas (with Clear Facilitators)

If I was king of meetings for a day, I would create two rules. The first would be that you don't get to request a meeting without an agenda. The second would be that you don't get to ask for a meeting when it's not clear who the facilitator is.

Those two things are intimately connected because if they are not set, we're back to the "somebody" problem. Somebody will figure out the agenda, and somebody will lead the conversation. But when we all log in to the video call at 11 a.m. Team Standard Time, "somebody" hasn't shown up to lead the meeting.

My rule is that if you call the meeting, you are the facilitator. If you want the meeting, it's now your job to come up with the agenda and drive the conversation. This is considerably harder than most people think, which means that in the future, they might find another way to obtain that information than a meeting.

Thinking about meeting blocks makes the job much easier for both the facilitator and the rest of us who are showing up. If you tell me the meeting is to "talk about" Project X, I don't know what I need to do to prepare. If I know the meeting is so that we can come to a decision on Project X, I know exactly what is expected of me when I show up.

As well as assigning a facilitator, it can also be useful to assign other meeting roles, such as a scribe for note-taking and a timekeeper who can keep an eye on the clock and make sure enough time is left for alignment and next steps.

Meeting Templates

Much of the work for the facilitator is thinking through how they'll lead the conversation effectively. One way to solve that issue quickly is to use meeting templates. Meeting templates don't have to be restrictive; they can simply be a rough agenda template that has the key building blocks for certain types of meetings baked in.

For example, most team meetings need some time for grounding and bonding before diving into the meat of the agenda, so it makes sense for that to be a standard block on the agenda. But you can approach that bonding block in a number of ways. You could leave it as open water-cooler time, where people take a few minutes to chat about their weekend at the Monday-morning update meeting. You could make it more structured, where everyone has a minute to answer an icebreaker question.

At Team PF, we start our monthly update meeting by asking for everyone's wins and celebrations. This has the benefit of starting the meeting with some lightness and levity and gives us a chance to learn what everyone else has been up to. It's also an incredibly powerful way to kick off the rest of the meeting with forward momentum and confidence.

If you're scheduling a problem-solving meeting, you might start with an update block to get everyone on the same page. Next, you might have a brainstorming session, followed by a planning block and then the next steps. Instead of repeatedly rebuilding that agenda from scratch, create a meeting template that anyone who is facilitating can use whenever your team needs to solve a problem.

As a side benefit, creating or reconstructing meeting templates can be a powerful opportunity to think together as a team about all the other things that you do outside the meeting.

For example, when we created our template for team development meetings (our spin on performance reviews), it made us rethink how we wanted to approach the entire review process. Typically, a performance review is top down, with your boss coming in and telling you whether or not you're doing great. At Team PF, we decided to invert that model and create a container for the team members to tell their manager how things are going and bring up hard conversations they might need to have.

Our team development meeting has several key parts:

- We talk about what you've done well over the most recent period of time.
- We ask what internal challenges you're having (e.g., you don't have your schedule properly aligned for your chronotype).
- We ask what external blockers have made it difficult for you to work (e.g., team priorities are unclear or in conflict).
- We ask if there are any hard conversations that you need to have with your manager or as a team.
- We ask what you are interested in focusing on in the future.

Creating this template allowed us to reshape the typical performance review and turn it into a meeting that increases belonging, proactively addresses hard conversations, and builds excitement for the future.

ROCKET PRACTICE

BUILD MEETING TEMPLATES

» What types of meetings do you have most frequently? Think in terms of different time horizons: daily, weekly, monthly, quarterly, and annually. Don't worry about capturing all of them in your first pass. If your time is limited, start by thinking about your daily and weekly recurring meetings.

» Pick two to three kinds of meetings to work on first, and review the building blocks you use. What blocks could you add to improve the meeting (for example, a bonding block at the beginning of the meeting)? What blocks could you subtract (for example, an update block that could be an email)?

» Share your proposed meeting template with your team in advance of the next meeting. Don't surprise your team in real time with a brand-new way of doing things; take advantage of the IKEA effect and get buy-in by inviting them to help you create a better meeting structure.

» Give your team three to five runs of the new meeting template before you decide to make too many changes to it. That will help you dial in how much time you actually need per building block and give you a sense of what other team habits are being displaced or absorbed by the new meeting structure.

» As you begin to audit your meetings, start to build a library of templates. What should be in your weekly huddle? What can you add that would make it more powerful? What can you subtract? (You will find examples of meeting templates at teamhabitsbook .com/resources.)

MAKE THE DEFAULT "NO INVITE"

Once you start thinking about meeting math, it quickly becomes clear that a teamwide meeting request for thirty minutes is a way bigger ask than many of us have been led to think. Maybe you've concluded that the meeting is still necessary—but does everyone on the team need to be there?

We've already discussed several reasons why you might not invite someone to a meeting. In the chapter on belonging, we discussed intentional exclusion as a kindness you can do for your coworkers. In the chapter on goal-setting and prioritization, we talked about how people who are wearing the green hat (meaning in the middle of high-priority work on a project) may not need to attend a meeting that would sidetrack them from their work.

As a meeting facilitator, it's your job to ask who else doesn't belong on your invite list.

Unlike culling people from your holiday soiree, dropping people from a work meeting that they don't need to attend is a kindness. And when your team habit is that your default is no invite, it becomes a forcing function to make sure that every person you invite to every meeting has a clear reason for needing to be there.

If the reason for a person's attendance isn't clear, do one of two things:

- Let them know they don't need to be at the meeting and tell them why. For example, the meeting will focus on approving graphic assets for a launch, and their part of the project doesn't involve the graphics.
- Think through the meeting agenda and revise it so that their contribution is clear. For example, even though their part of the project doesn't involve the graphics, you need to tap their technical expertise so that the final graphics play nicely with the marketing automation software that person manages.

"You need to stay informed" isn't a fantastic reason for your teammate to be at a meeting. It's not *incorrect*—they do need to stay informed. But if you send an update email at the end of the meeting, that teammate can skim it in five minutes and be able to stay on track with their workday.

When the default is no invite, the result is that anyone who's at the meeting has a purpose for being there and knows what it is. This gives your teammates the gift of being able to be fully engaged in the meeting versus either showing up without being prepared to contribute or attending under duress while thinking about the work they could be doing instead.

The inverse team habit is to make it possible for individual teammates to ask why they need to be at a meeting if they're unsure. They shouldn't ask in a hostile way but rather to obtain clarity and context about how they'll contribute.

There is an exception to the "default is no invite" rule: bonding meetings. If people are especially busy, it's easy to assume that because they're on a high-priority project, they probably shouldn't be spending their time at meetings unrelated to the work at hand. True. But in that case, I would suggest delaying the bonding meeting until every team member can be there.

This respects the time of the team member who is wearing the green hat *without* also giving the impression that bonding actually isn't important. Even if we don't explicitly say so, excluding busy team members from a bonding session tells everyone that the work itself is more important than coming together as a team.

ROCKET PRACTICE

WHY AM I AT THIS MEETING?

- » For every person who is invited to a meeting, write one to three sentences to explain why their presence is required. Bonus points if you share it with your teammates so they can come prepared to fully participate.
- » Create a team habit where every team member can ask for clarification about why they should be at a meeting so that they can either become a better team player by participating in the meeting or get back to work that is a more valuable use of their time and attention.
- » If the purpose of the meeting is primarily bonding, delay it until everyone on the team is able to attend.

CAPTURE NEXT STEPS

In theory, we all know that it doesn't make sense to have an entire meeting and then walk away without going over the next steps. *Of course* we should capture our ideas at the end of the meeting and turn our decisions into action points.

In practice, we are probably not doing it as well as we could.

The main reason is that our meetings are crammed with different building blocks, and we simply don't leave ourselves the last five to ten minutes to process what needs to happen. Why does this become a problem?

- The context in which we are having the meeting differs from the context in which we will be doing the work, and details will inevitably be missed in the transfer. For example, we may be brainstorming in Google Docs or on a whiteboard in the conference room. But that space probably isn't also where we keep track of team tasks and draft work, so unless one of us converts these notes into tasks in a team channel, the work we did disappears.
- We expect individual participants to keep track of their own next steps. I have my list and you have your list, but because there's no central source of truth, there's nothing to keep us from drifting. We decided on the call that we are going to California, but because it's not written down, neither of us realizes that I meant Sacramento while you were thinking San Diego.
- It seems pretty clear who's doing what, so you don't bring it up. *Or* you have no idea who will own the action item, but it will take so long to figure it out that it seems easier to just not do so. Either way, "somebody" ends up with the task because we didn't take the time to assign it.

In an ideal world, you leave the meeting with fewer open loops than you started with. Not adequately dealing with next steps means that even if your meeting closed a few loops, it opened up even more.

 ROCKET PRACTICE

DEFINE NEXT STEPS

While it's always a good team habit to practice properly capturing and assigning next steps, there are a few cases in which you need to be especially clear. You might have a new teammate who does not have the same high-level context about how you do things around here. Or maybe you just switched collaborative technology and need to remind people not to look at the old team wiki but to go check the Notion board instead. You could be in the middle of a major context or priority shift or a high-urgency event, such as a launch, and some of your team habits may have shifted or been suspended.

Even if you're not in any of those situations, you may know that next steps and action items are being lost. If so, this team habit needs to shift.

» When you set the agenda for a meeting, leave five to ten minutes for capturing next actions and designate one person to add those action items to the team collaboration space. (Remember from the last chapter, teamwork needs to happen in team channels.)

» For each action item, include these four elements:

1. What is the action item?
2. Who owns it?
3. Where does it live?
4. When will we see it show up in that spot?

» If you sense that you need to make a radical change around how you capture next steps, schedule a separate meeting to discuss it. That way, you're not trying to figure it out while distracting from the topic of another regular meeting. Using the meeting blocks, design a meeting specifically to address changing this team habit.

CHAPTER 9 TAKEAWAYS

- Meetings can be either a powerful force multiplier or a powerful force diminisher, which is why they're a good place to start when it comes to changing team habits.
- Every meeting has hidden costs. A one-hour meeting with five team members actually takes up ninety minutes per team member. What could your team do with an extra seven and a half hours a week?

- Every meeting should have a facilitator and an agenda.
- Use the six meeting blocks (decision-making, planning, brainstorming, bonding, review, and update) to build better meetings and create meeting templates.
- Everyone who attends a meeting should have a clearly defined reason for being there. Otherwise, the default should be no invite.
- Leave time at the end of every meeting to capture next steps.

CORE TEAM HABITS

TEN

Individually, we are one drop.
Together, we are an ocean.

—Ryunosuke Satoro

I've called the team the atomic element of the organization, and so far, the focus of this book has been on how that atom functions as a whole. In this chapter, I will zero in on the protons, neutrons, and electrons that make up a team: the individuals.

With Army training, required skills are broken into three parts: common soldier skills, collective skills, and unit skills—in other words, the skills you need to learn at an individual level, those you need as a squad, and those you need at the platoon, company, or greater level. The reason we train in these different echelons is because if a soldier can't master common soldier skills, they won't be able to execute the collective exercises—and they certainly won't be able to do the higher-level things that will be required of them as part of a unit.

It's similar in a workplace team. As individuals working together, we need to practice a few core skills in order to collaborate, communicate, and show up to do our best work for our team.

SHOW YOUR WORK

There are three ways in which I mean show your work: show how you got there, show your status as you go, and show something for your time. All of these support the habit of opening the black box, which we talked about in the chapter on collaboration.

Show How You Got from A to Z

This hearkens back to middle school math, where Ms. Gonzales, your algebra teacher, told you to show how you solved an equation so she could see how well you understood the principles and reasoning. In a team setting, showing how you got from A to Z means rather than making a brilliant leap and leaving your teammates mystified about how you arrived there, build a habit of bringing them along in the process.

This is important for a few reasons. First, it helps demystify brilliance in a way that supports the team. Some members of the team may seem supernaturally brilliant at a certain task. They have an idea or are assigned a task, and two weeks later, they come back with a completed artifact. While that's fantastic, it can also create a situation in which no one else feels that they can participate in that type of project.

The good news is that there are almost always incremental steps on the path to a final product, and brilliant people can usually show you how they got there—even if it takes time to explain. When we build the team habit of explaining how we accomplish our work, we end up sharing resources, building models and frameworks, and helping create more resilient, less fragile team members who can support each other more fully.

The other reason it's important to show how you got from A to Z is that it creates a team that can act as a good sounding board or check. When your teammates understand how you work, they can support you better. You can bounce ideas off them, and they can act as guardrails to make sure you're not working from faulty or out-of-date assumptions.

Show Early Drafts

Rather than waiting to share your work until it's completed, get in the habit of showing drafts or prototypes as you go along. This allows the team to see where the work is without having to ask as well as to catch problems earlier and support you in areas where you might be struggling.

Sharing early drafts requires trust and is a place where shortcodes and clear communication can go a long way. Is this early draft for visibility only, or are you ready for feedback? What level of feedback would help you at this stage? Do you want just broad structural or conceptual comments, or do you need an eagle eye for hunting typos?

I'm not saying you need to compose every draft in a shared Google document with your teammates' icons popping in and out of the upper right corner. Few can do their best work with someone watching over their shoulder. Work in focus blocks with your door closed, but be prepared to open it regularly to share early stages of your work.

One of the great things about showing your work in this way is that you learn to give your team and yourself bread crumbs.

When you know someone else will see an early draft or prototype, you start leaving comments to explain the status of certain sections. You might note what needs additional work or point out places where you're blocked or need additional information. Not only does this help the viewer understand what stage your draft is on, it also means that if you need to step away from the project for some reason, you won't be completely lost when you return.

When leaving bread crumbs in an early draft, don't write cryptic notes that only you can decipher. Just as we discussed in the collaboration chapter regarding writing tasks and action items, write bread crumbs as though you're writing to someone who has no idea what's going on.

Show Something for Your Time

Finally, showing your work reduces much of the metachatter that can happen around the work itself. As a team, we can spend a lot of time talking about the status of a project rather than working on it.

When you develop a habit of showing your work, your team can see that there's a physical or digital artifact instead of just a continual stream of status updates. Instead of talking about the report that you're writing, spend the time writing a draft to run by your team.

The habit of showing your work is a forcing function for a lot of other core team habits. When people know how you got from A to Z, they can support you more fully. When you've left bread crumbs, your team members can take over in a pinch and help you move the project forward. When they see a digital or physical artifact of the work, they can spend their time communicating about topics that are more impactful than work status updates.

ROCKET PRACTICE

START SHOWING YOUR WORK

- » How does your team currently share their work? What can be changed to provide more insight into how tasks and projects are happening and where projects get stuck or need additional support?
- » What is the Goldilocks zone of showing progress via deliverables that allows people's work to be seen and celebrated without inundating the team with review and approval cycles?

» What are the tasks and projects that seem to be the most dependent upon one person? How might a team and that person show how the work is done so that more teammates learn what is entailed and can support that task or project?

» What needs to shift so that your team feels comfortable sharing prototypes, drafts, and early works in progress? How can this become a positive, proactive norm versus something you do only when a teammate or manager asks?

USE FOCUS BLOCKS TO GET REAL ABOUT YOUR CAPACITY AND PRIORITIZATION

In *Start Finishing*, I discuss the four basic blocks that we can build into our days: focus blocks, social blocks, admin blocks, and recovery blocks. Focus blocks are the engine of our most important work, those ninety-minute to two-hour blocks of time where we're especially creative and inspired. This is where we can do our deep work and stay focused enough on a project to move it forward or complete it.

We're conditioned to chop our workdays into one-hour blocks. So why define focus blocks as ninety minutes to two hours? Because an hour just doesn't go as far as people think it does. You need time to get into the work, time to run at your most focused and creative, and time to wind back down and move to another project. That ninety-minute to two-hour block of time accommodates the warm-up–focus–wind-down attention cycle that feels natural to many people.

When you start thinking in terms of focus blocks, you also acquire a fantastic tool for project estimation. Most of us are terrible at estimating how long something will take, especially when we're talking about minutes. We're very bad at estimating what we can accomplish in five minutes or even an hour. But even at a team level, we're surprisingly good at estimating what a team or an individual can do with a solid focus block.

We know what we can accomplish if we go dark for a working session, and as a result, we can become pretty good at estimating how many focus blocks it will take to accomplish certain projects. Instead of calculating hours, we can start using focus blocks as the fundamental building block of a project plan. For a standard project, your team can develop a sense that Janie needs three focus blocks for her part, Antonio and Carmen two coworking blocks for their part, and Mei Lin a final block for her review pass.

Thinking in focus blocks also makes this truth painfully clear: When you have too few (or no) focus blocks, work doesn't get done. And most teams that I consult with have far too few focus blocks for the amount of work on their plate.

How Many Focus Blocks Do You Have?

Just as we had meeting math in the last chapter, we also need to talk about focus-block math.

When you're considering a new project, you need to think critically about how many focus blocks you have available. If you are like most teams, you're probably already at capacity. Which, as we talked about with the 85 Percent Rule in the planning chapter, technically means that you're overburdened.

My standing rule is that you need three focus blocks per week per project in order to make progress. You need multiple deep work passes throughout the week to get anywhere on that next marketing campaign, figure out your staffing strategy, or change shipping vendors.

That said, every team will take a different amount of time to accomplish a task, depending on their readiness level and performance. Each teammate will take a different amount of time. The more you work with focus blocks, the better you'll become at estimating how many you and your team will need for your most common projects.

Take a look at your schedule. How many focus blocks do you have available? You might find space for ten, but how many of those are not already allocated or used by recurring or urgent work? When you account for recurring and urgent work, most teams go from ten available focus blocks to two—if they're lucky.

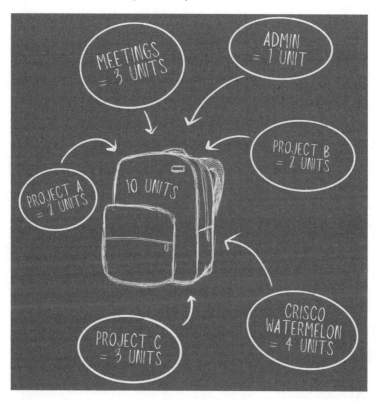

If you know those remaining two focus blocks are spoken for by a current project and that this new project will require four weekly focus blocks, the math is clear. You can't fit fourteen units of stuff into a ten-unit bag, which means that you need to create some new units, drop some of the projects you're currently doing, or become quicker, because right now, there's just not enough of a window of opportunity to take on something new.

When you take focus-block math seriously, it becomes a catalytic conversation. You start to see very clearly where people have time to get work done in their schedules, and you'll likely realize it's not just one person who is short on time and running behind—your whole team is probably short on focus blocks.

You might also start to realize how many of those focus blocks are happening in the evenings or on weekends. If your meeting schedule has made Swiss cheese of your teammates' daily schedules, evenings and weekends might be the only time they can do deeper work.

Constantly taking work home is demoralizing and frustrating on an individual level. It can also be extremely inequitable at a team level.

Certain teammates—whether because of their roles or societal norms— probably carry a lot of the emotional labor for the team throughout the workday, which means their schedules are eaten up by other people's priorities. They end up taking work home—but in many cases, they're probably also doing emotional labor at home while trying to fit in the conceptual labor of work they weren't able to accomplish during the day.

When we open up our team's calendar and start talking about focus blocks, it can provide a unique window on when work is actually being done and by who. And hopefully, it can open up a wider conversation about how we can better protect *all* our teammates' time so they have the space to do their best work at the best time rather than taking it home because they have no other option.

Free Up Focus Blocks

As a team, when we can come together and be brutally honest about how many focus blocks we actually have, we can make better choices about how to solve the problem. Maybe we need to become faster and more efficient with the time available. Maybe we need to reallocate work around the team. Maybe we can cut some TIMWOOD waste (see Chapter 8) or remove a standing meeting from the schedule (see Chapter 9).

Focus-block math is the inverse of meeting math. Where adding a single meeting to the schedule ties up exponential hours, adding a focus block to everyone's schedules can be an incredible force multiplier. If we as a team realize that we have only two focus blocks for strategic work every week, and we figure out how to open up another two focus blocks a week per teammate, we've doubled our capacity to do our best work.

Other people in the organization will notice. Once your team starts doubling their capacity for strategic work, you'll probably find that your team is assigned more projects. When you knock those out of the park, people around you will start to ask what you're doing differently.

This is one of the powerful ways a team can lead by example—and ultimately shape an organization—that we talked about in Chapter 1.

COWORKING FOCUS BLOCKS

In a team setting, a focus block does not necessarily have to be solo work time. You might be better served by working together with a coworker on a common problem.

Coworking blocks are essentially project-focused meetings. They follow the rules of focus blocks, but they also follow some of the rules of meetings and often use the same meeting blocks we talked about in the last chapter. However, even if there's an agenda, they tend to be a lot looser. You might quickly flip between deciding and brainstorming and reviewing and bonding—think of coworking sessions as more jazzy than orchestral.

The best coworking sessions have a dedicated facilitator (at least a light facilitator) who keeps track of things like how much time is left, what we are doing next, where we are in the project, and what we should be working on right now. Their job is to keep the coworking session from going off the rails and ensure that we're making the best use of our time.

This is where the doer-reviewer-coordinator triad that we talked about in Chapter 8 can come into play. If you have a coworking session that involves your entire triad, the doer and reviewer will probably be playing creative hacky sack with each other while the coordinator acts as the implicit facilitator. This works well because the coordinator is the one who will need to report on the work that happened in the session so the people who were not part of the hacky-sack game understand what's happening.

If the coordinator is not part of the coworking session, the reviewer usually becomes the de facto facilitator because the doer most likely has their hands so deep in the work that they're hyperfocused. Asking them to sustain the structure of the meeting at the same time can be counterproductive.

Honor Focus Blocks

It's one thing to find open focus blocks on your team's calendar. It's another thing entirely to *keep* them open.

If we have a meeting starting at 1 p.m., we'll make sure we're back from our lunch breaks in time or say, "Sorry, I'm about to head into a meeting" if a teammate asks for help with a "quick favor." It's much harder to block off time if it's "just" for a focus block.

Many teams either don't put focus blocks on their calendar (which means these blocks are eaten up by the "open time = free to meet" norm) or pencil them into the day in such a way that they're easy to move if a meeting comes up. Either way, the end result is that the team members don't actually have focus blocks to work with.

The second scenario is often more demoralizing than not putting the focus blocks on the calendar in the first place. It's hard enough work to schedule a focus block; moving it becomes a broken promise to oneself.

This is why it's important to not only identify focus blocks but also schedule them on the calendar and honor them, just as you would a meeting.

As a team, develop the habit of honoring each others' focus blocks. "I have a focus block to work on Project X" should be every bit as valid as "I have a meeting" when it comes to saying no to other people's priorities.

Focus Blocks and Chronotypes

As we talked about in the meetings chapter, *when* you schedule those focus blocks is every bit as important as scheduling them. Are you setting yourself up for your best work according to your chronotype? Or are you constantly struggling in an uphill effort by scheduling deep work when your energy is lowest?

In Daniel H. Pink's book *When: The Scientific Secrets of Perfect Timing*,[1] he writes about the hidden effects of chronotypes on our lives. If you meet with a judge after lunch or when they are tired, you're statistically more likely to receive a harsh judgment than if you meet with them when they are full and happy in the morning. The scenario is the same for doctors and surgeons: The number of mistakes that happen in an afternoon surgery means that even if you're not a morning person, you should still do what you can to get those early appointments.

Your team may not be handing out life sentences or brain surgeries, but your chronotypes still affect the work that you do together and separately. You do your best work when you're energized, not when you're tired or hungry and distracted by the internal debate between getting a burrito or going for Thai.

Most of us fall into three categories: morning larks, afternoon emus, and night owls, although in *The Power of When*,[2] sleep expert Michael Breus identified a fourth chronotype, dolphins, whose bursts of creative energy tend to be scattered throughout the day.

Knowing your chronotype can help you schedule focus blocks when they work best for you throughout the day as well as identifying when throughout the week your energy tends to be at its best. Creating a team habit of knowing and working with your teammates' chronotypes can help you identify patterns and push work forward by handing it off at times that are optimal for all of you.

At a daily level: If you know that your creative energy flags in the late afternoon, it's probably best to schedule things that need high energy and concentration—such as deep work and brainstorming meetings— when you're more alert. Coordinate with your teammates to ensure that you're passing off your parts of the project to them during their own creative peaks.

At a weekly level: Pay attention to how your energy flows throughout the week. For example, I am typically energetically great Monday through Wednesday. I start flagging Thursday and Friday. Conversely, my teammate Shannon shares Garfield's view of Mondays, but by Wednesday, she's on fire. When we're collaborating on a project, we're most effective when I make sure that I have pushed my part as far as I can by Wednesday so that Shannon can pick up the baton and take it through the end of the week.

AUDIT YOUR FOCUS BLOCKS

» Without looking at people's schedules, write down how many total focus blocks you think your team has per week to focus on their best work. Break down your estimate per teammate. Then, have a conversation with your teammates about how many focus blocks they *actually* have per week. Notice any discrepancies between their responses and your estimate.

» Which one habit category in this book would open up the most focus blocks for the most members of your team? Meetings and collaboration are great places to start looking for habits to shift.

» Discuss with your team what kind of projects or activities they would most like to focus on should they get more focus blocks back. Think in terms of both individual projects and collective projects that your team might pursue going forward.

» How will you honor your focus blocks? How will you add them to your individual and team schedules? How will you empower teammates to protect focus blocks from meeting requests and other priorities that might try to creep in?

» What is your chronotype, and when do you do your best work? In working with your team, how can you shift focus blocks or work to free people of different chronotypes to do their best work? How can you pair people with different chronotypes to better pass work between teammates?

SHOOT, MOVE, COMMUNICATE

A recurring mantra in Army training is "Shoot! Move! Communicate!" It was so ingrained that when it came time to shoot, every soldier reflexively knew what to do.

It seems to be about firing weapons, but it's really about everything you do: **Take an action, move to a better position, tell people what**

you've done and where you are. That lets them know what their next action, move, and communication needs to be.

This habit is particularly important in a fast-moving team, whether in person or virtual. When things are moving quickly, it's easy to get out of sync. To avoid duplicated work, ghost plans (Chapter 6), Crisco watermelons (Chapter 2), and all the daily bumps that happen in a fast-moving team, we need team habits that allow team members to take initiative, drive work forward, and then proactively communicate about what they've done.

Were I to translate so that it didn't invoke firing weapons, I might say "Ship! Move! Communicate!" But notice that the same discipline is used in sports. Whether it's "Ship! Move! Communicate!" or "Shoot! Move! Communicate!," we'll all be best served by returning to one of those mantras multiple times a day to prompt us to do all three.

What does this look like in the workplace?

- Shoot: When you see a problem, create a plan to fix it.
- Move: Fix it or call the Wolf (Chapter 8) who can.
- Communicate: Tell people what you've done and provide a status update.

Shoot! Move! Communicate! invites you to not just slap a Band-Aid on a project and move on but to own the problem and take responsibility for fixing it and closing the loop. Part of doing that well is understanding that there are almost always two levels of fix for any problem that comes up.

The Local Fix

When a customer writes in to complain about a particular problem with your app, service, or product, your level 1 fix is to solve the customer's problem quickly and immediately.

The Global or System Fix

What upstream process or system created the customer's problem to begin with? How can you solve that before it causes problems for more customers down the road?

If you're shooting, moving, and communicating, you will

- **Shoot:** Take the initiative to solve the customer's problem.
- **Move:** Go deeper to find the defect in the process that caused the problem.
- **Communicate:** Let the team know what you did to solve the level 1 problem, and what your DRIP (see the communication chapter) is to solve the level 2 problem.

As a general principle, start by solving the local fix and then look for a global or system fix. In this example, even if you're busy behind the scenes solving the problem the customer reached out about, if you haven't reached out to the customer to let them know, their frustration is probably rising. Don't get trapped working on the global systemic fix while leaving the initial problem burning in the corner.

Learning to look for both fixes is an excellent team habit to build. It can be very frustrating when a teammate simply takes care of the customer but doesn't do anything to fix the upstream problem that caused the customer complaint (or at least elevate it to the right person). That just leads to the team being inundated with the same problem again and again.

One of the reasons broken printers often exist is because someone stopped after the level 1 fix. They put the broken printer in the closet or on the chair in the conference room and then dusted off their hands and went on their way. Because nobody looked for a level 2 fix, the printer remained a constant annoyance in the corner.

ROCKET PRACTICE

SHOOT, MOVE, COMMUNICATE

» Think about the common kinds of problems your team runs into. How do you communicate about the first fix? What is the process for identifying and solving the second fix? How do you communicate about that?

» What problems have emerged that had a level 1 fix but didn't have a level 2 fix? What is your team's plan for capturing those and solving them?

» What needs to shift in your team's habits so that everyone can address level 1 problems when they see them? What needs to shift so that more people can really address that level 2 fix rather than those solutions being bottlenecked by one or two people?

ELIMINATE YOUR ACHILLES HEEL BY ILLUMINATING IT

All of us have weak spots. You could be a fantastic presenter with a terrible eye for slide design. You might be incredible at orchestrating all the moving pieces of a team project but painfully disorganized when it comes to your own to-do list. Or maybe you're a whiz at solving customer problems but have an impossible time having hard conversations with teammates.

Each of us has an area where we don't shine as brightly as we'd like. That's just part of being human. It's when you try to hide that weakness—whether out of pride, a desire to excel, or fear of ridicule—that it becomes an Achilles heel.

The good news is that you don't need to walk around with a potentially fatal chink in your armor. **Instead of ignoring or hiding your own Achilles heel, you can convert it from a weakness into a strength by telling the team about it.**

To paraphrase one of my favorite lines from the Tao Te Ching, "Because the sage is aware of her faults, she is faultless." If Achilles had been aware of (or less prideful about) his vulnerable heel, he might have protected it. If you are willing to be vulnerable about your own weaknesses with your team, you will effectively prevent those weaknesses from becoming a problem.

If you struggle in silence rather than telling your team you have an Achilles heel, it ends up looking like you can't ship or perform overall. Your team or manager probably won't see that you and spreadsheets get along like oil and water—instead, they're going to think you can't do your entire job.

Meanwhile, someone else on the team might be a rock star at the thing you keep stumbling over or truly love the task you hate. Struggling in silence is keeping them from their own chance to shine.

It takes a lot of trust in belonging to admit vulnerability, but the highest-performing teams are those who know each other's strengths and weaknesses so thoroughly that they can support each other through any task. As a team, we can create a team Achilles heel map where we note everyone's strengths *and* weaknesses and brainstorm ways to support each other more fully.

For example, if we know you're straight-up terrible with spreadsheets, we can spend some time training you or pair you with someone who's a spreadsheet whiz. Or if we know sales is not your forte, we know better than to assign you the task of closing a deal. However, we could make you the project owner, where your job is to call the right Wolf to help you get the job done.

The thing about eliminating your Achilles heel is that somebody on the team has to take the first step. It's a huge courage point. A person has to be vulnerable to say, "I'm not good at this thing."

We all need to practice asking for help, *and* many of us need to practice sharing our hidden superpowers. All of us have an Achilles heel, and asking for help with our particular weakness opens up the opportunity for us to help our teammates with things that might be our strong suits.

The result is that we create shifts of energy around our weak points so that—as a team—we can cover for, support, and uplift each other. If you're willing to lead the change, illuminating your Achilles heels as a team can be an incredible catalyst for performance and belonging.

 ROCKET PRACTICE

CREATE AN ACHILLES HEEL MAP

» If you have a high-trust team, suggest a discussion about this issue in one of your upcoming meetings. This is both a bonding and a brainstorming block where you can share your Achilles heels and hidden superpowers and help come up with solutions to support your teammates.

» In a lower-trust team, start by sharing your Achilles heel with one or two people on your team who you trust. They'll probably share theirs with you, too. Over time, you can grow your fledgling map of Achilles heels and hidden superpowers as your team's trust grows.

» When building small teams or project teams, be intentional about adding people who complement or can counter your Achilles heel. Even if they're not officially on your project team, you can tap their expertise by including them in coworking sessions.

» Whenever you hear a teammate mention a weakness or Achilles heel, thank them for sharing it. This starts to build a team culture in which it's not dangerous to reveal weaknesses and in which you know you can reach out for help if you need it.

LEARN HOW TO HELP YOUR TEAMMATES WHEN THEY FALL BEHIND

Since we're admitting to being human in this chapter, we also need to acknowledge that humans fall behind.

We get sick. Unforeseen things pop up. We are assigned a strategic project on a tight timeline because leadership didn't apply the 3x Rule that we talked about in the planning chapter. Priorities shift, new goals appear, the economy turns upside down.

Working in a team means that if one of your teammates is behind, it puts the rest of you behind. And the reality is that at least one of you will be behind at any given moment. That's the nature of work.

Unfortunately, instead of embracing the reality that people fall behind and developing team habits to help them catch up, many team cultures create a pressure cooker of continual anxiety in which being behind is so unacceptable that it creates a compounding level of stress. (Which tends to put people even more behind.) When that's the status quo, it leads to burnout and resignations.

We need to normalize the fact that we all fall behind and build team habits to support us when we do. And it turns out there are more and less constructive ways to offer help.

Too often, when we see a teammate is behind, we assume they need us to either jump in to help or take things off their plate. These interventions normally come from good intentions, but they can often make the problem worse. It's hard enough to catch up without everyone fussing about you or feeling like a failure because your teammates have taken work away.

This is especially the case if a teammate has fallen behind because of life stuff. Our first instinct is often to tell that teammate not to worry about work projects or to reassign some of their work to someone else. But many people feel a sense of contribution, meaning, and purpose at work. If they're experiencing duress in their personal life, work might be the only thing helping them hang on. Taking work off their plate can actually make matters worse.

If we shouldn't immediately jump in or take work away, how can we help our teammates when they fall behind?

The first step is to eliminate any penalties for people who fall behind. Instead, try to figure out what happened. I've been in a leadership position long enough to know that when my team is behind, it's often because of upstream choices I have made. Sometimes it isn't clear what being on track means. A ghost plan might be in play, or perhaps no one is on the same page about timelines, expectations, and schedule because of bad communication habits. Or it could be that the team doesn't have clarity about who's on first or who's making decisions.

Once you've looked at the root cause, you can start looking for solutions.

Before you proactively start generating "solutions" for your teammate, I will suggest something far simpler and more powerful: **Ask them what they need, and be prepared to provide it.**

Setting up some of the team habits we've already talked about in this chapter will make this easier. First, it will give you all a common language. Your teammate can say, "I'm behind because I have six focus blocks' worth of work to do each week and only two free blocks per week." Or "I'm behind because it turns out this task is an Achilles heel for me, and I need to call in a Wolf."

Maybe your teammate needs to ask for the green hat for the rest of the week to catch up instead of attending a bunch of meetings. Maybe they thrive on social processing and coworking and have been struggling to do a task solo that they would flash through in one or two coworking focus blocks.

We tend to think of support as something we need to add: resources, hands on deck, oversight. Often, we should be asking what we need to subtract: meetings, repetitive work, responsibilities that shouldn't have been on that person's plate to begin with.

ROCKET PRACTICE

SUPPORT TEAMMATES

» If your teammate has not proactively said they're behind, start by having a conversation with them about where they think they are with the project and whether it is on track. Once you have alignment on the status of the work, start brainstorming solutions for catching up.

» Rather than coming up with solutions for your teammate, *ask* what support they need. More importantly, be prepared to provide resources for that support. Keep in mind that support could be either the addition of something or the subtraction of something. Maybe they need additional budget; maybe they need to skip a few meetings this week. Keep in mind that sometimes a teammate won't know what they need. Ask more specific, guiding questions to help them articulate what would support them.

» If the whole team isn't already in the know, ask your teammate for permission to tell the rest of the team they're behind and what support they need. Your teammate may prefer to bring this up themselves, or they might appreciate you providing covering fire so that they can get on with their work.

GIVE DIRECT FEEDBACK

As we talked about in the chapter on belonging, there will always be bumps when humans are moving quickly together. The fact of the matter is that sometimes you need to give folks some direct feedback. It might be tough feedback. It might be good feedback that's tough to hear. It might be constructive feedback. However you label it, it can be awkward to share direct feedback with a coworker.

Because of this, many teams develop the bad habit of avoiding talking about bumps. When they have feedback, they try to sneak it across to their peer by roping in a manager or another teammate. This creates an uncomfortable triangle where the person who was roped in isn't sure why they were, and it puts additional work onto someone else's shoulders.

Worse, the teammate who needs to receive the feedback probably feels betrayed.

Most people would prefer that you come talk to them directly, and not doing so erodes their trust and violates the very fact that your true team is only the four to eight people who you work with regularly.

Additionally, whenever you escalate something to another person in the chain, you're using up a little bit of your team's belonging and trust—as well as some of your team's organizational social capital. The more your team can take care of its own business, the more you and your teammates can be free to continue building better team habits together.

I want to add the caveat that if you feel physically unsafe or if you're in a place where giving feedback will create retribution of any kind, this becomes an HR issue. But when we're talking about the normal everyday bumps of teammates who otherwise know, like, and trust each other, then it's important to build the team habit of giving direct feedback well.

Check Your Timing

If your teammate is in the middle of a stressful day or you're all in a pressure cooker of a project, you may want to wait for a better time to bring up the bump. Or you may need to take a few days to figure out how to articulate what you're trying to say.

But don't wait too long. If you let something stew before bringing it up, it has the unintended effect of making the recipient of the feedback think you've been holding on to the issue for a long time. They'll assume that it's weightier than it might actually be.

Provide Context

No one likes to get a message that says only "Hey, can we talk?" It's too easy to go to the worst-case scenario only to find out that your teammate wants you to CC them on certain conversations.

When you talk about the bump, preface it by describing the specific incident, explaining why it didn't land well with you, and asking your questions about it.

Focus on Understanding

Remember, you're not setting up this conversation to accuse your teammate. Instead, you're there to listen and understand. You might find that you completely misunderstood the situation and ended up making up a story about the event.

This conversation shouldn't be about asserting power or imposing your will on someone else. It's about building a common bridge with a teammate who you spend time with, day in and day out. Before assigning ill intention to their action, give them the benefit of the doubt.

Think of the Best-Case Scenario

Too many people—peers and managers alike—put off hard conversations because they're worried about the worst-case scenario. What if I hurt her feelings? What if he never forgives me? What if they don't want to work with me anymore?

But these are the types of conversations that tend to bring a higher level of belonging in a team. They can bring you closer together as teammates and help your team achieve even more together.

Stop focusing on the worst-case scenario and start imagining the best-case scenario, where you resolve a bump and gain a higher level of trust. Spoiler alert: That's often the most likely outcome.

 **ROCKET PRACTICE**

GIVING DIRECT FEEDBACK

» If you need to give constructive feedback to a teammate, give them the benefit of the doubt and use the language of bumps and team habits to talk about the practice, principle, or process that is causing friction.

» If you're a manager, ask your teammate if they've already spoken directly with their peer. If not, why not? If there's not a good reason—such as emotional or physical safety—then ask your teammate to resolve it on their own. You can coach them through the best ways to deliver feedback, but don't take that monkey from them (see Chapter 4) and become the de facto mediator for interpersonal issues.

» During your conversation, determine whether this bump was brought about by other team habits that the entire team might benefit from discussing together. Are there any broader implications that other teammates should be made aware of?

PERFORMANCE–BELONGING

Being in a team where you know you can ask for help and your team-mates will rally around you is an incredible feeling. It's empowering to know that you can accomplish hard tasks together, and every time you do it forges another link in the chain of belonging.

I've noted throughout this book how each category of habits builds on and influences other categories, and just because this book is written in a linear fashion doesn't mean that these core team habits constitute a finish line.

In a way, this chapter closes the open loop of our team habits categories by bringing us back to belonging. Just as belonging creates a foundation for better performance, performing well creates a foundation for belonging. That's the funny thing about systems: We often look for one-way causality when a system is actually a reciprocal feedback loop.

As you continue to work on team habits, keep noting where things shift in other categories, and celebrate the fact that you've taken one more step on a rewarding journey in which there's no limit to how bonded your team can be and how well they can perform.

CHAPTER 10 TAKEAWAYS

- To work best in a team, individuals need to practice certain core skills.
- Show your work: Show how you arrived at a finished product, show early drafts along the way, and show something for your time.
- Audit how many focus blocks your team has in their schedule, and use that as a measure for how much work you can accomplish.
- Shoot! Move! Communicate! Whenever you see a problem, create a plan to fix it; fix it or call the Wolf who can; and then communicate what you did.
- Practice identifying not just local fixes but also global or system fixes so you're not always dealing with the same problems.
- Convert your Achilles heel into a strength by creating the team habit of sharing your weaknesses and superpowers with the team.
- If a teammate falls behind, ask them what help they need before making assumptions.

ELEVEN

TEAM HABITS ARE POLITICAL— SO PLAY THE GAME

Change means that what was before wasn't perfect.
People want things to be better.

—Esther Dyson

Anyone who's ever tried to change a personal habit knows that it's a relatively simple process *and* that simple doesn't mean easy. Whether it's starting a new exercise regimen or reading before bed rather than scrolling through social media, our excitement about the idea only carries us so far. The new habit has to fight the Goliath of Inertia that comes from our existing behaviors.

My hope is that by now, you're fired up about changing some of your team's habits. You probably even have a few ideas about where to start. (More on that in a bit.) But just as with personal habit change, you will have to fight a long, uphill battle for even the simplest new team habit before it sticks. Not only is it facing the powerful Goliaths of team inertia and organizational stasis, but the social aspect of team habit change makes things even more complicated. Without alignment, this new team habit doesn't stand a chance.

When you embark on the journey of changing a team habit, you're changing an implicitly agreed-upon social behavior. And most of those implicitly agreed-upon social behaviors weren't solidified or maintained lately.

In Chapter 2, we talked about how to use the IKEA effect to your advantage by inviting your teammates into the process of building a new habit. Often, the status quo is a result of that same effect. We all worked together to get where we are, which means that even if it is not the most desirable option, we're still feeling the IKEA effect. There's still a lot of ego and sunk cost fallacy attached to the way we've always done things. Maybe it's not perfect, but it's *our* way.

When I come in for consultations to do this type of change work, I treat it as though I am walking onto someone else's land that they have been cultivating and tending. Even though I believe my suggestions will improve things considerably and that they'll be happy once I've done some work on the property, I also know you can't just walk onto somebody's land and start cutting down trees and moving fences without their consent.

It's helpful to have this metaphor in mind when making team habit changes. Existing team habits are there for a reason—even if they're no longer working for you. Your teammates have put some effort into tending this particular plot of land, and the first step in enrolling them in your vision of how to change it is to recognize and respect the work that came before.

When I say that team habits are political, I'm not talking about back-stabbing power plays, cliques, in-groups, or all the other negative connotations of workplace politics. Instead, I'm talking about the process of bringing a group of people together around a common initiative.

Team habit change is about alignment, not power. You're not trying to convince your teammates that your way is right or to win by having them choose your idea over someone else's. Instead, your goal should be to persuade each of your teammates to cocreate a vision with you. Adopting a new habit is hard enough. Doing the political work to align your team will make every step a bit easier. You'll face less resistance to your idea. You'll break through barriers more easily. And when things go off the rails (and they will), you will get back on track faster when you ask, "How did we get out of alignment?" rather than "Who is right or wrong?"

Aligning your team around the project is the only way to power change. But for your habit to have any chance of success, you need a champion.

WHO'S THE CHAMPION?

One of the reasons that broken printer has stayed parked on the third chair in the conference room for so long is that, as a team, we all figured that "somebody" would eventually take care of it. By this point in the book, you should know that "somebody" never does anything. Unless a champion steps up to rally everyone around this team habit change project, it will not happen.

If team habits are political, then the champion is the face of the campaign. They're the person who has the energy, desire for change, and stick-to-itiveness to see it through.

If your team has high belonging, your champion's job is straightforward. Your team is already aligned, and even if things don't go as planned—which we will talk about in the next chapter—your team will still be with you. They won't need additional alignment greasing.

If your a team has low belonging, your champion will have a tougher job. Remember, when it comes to team habit change, you don't win by beating opponents; you win by creating and enhancing partnerships with your allies. Your champion's job is to stay on that beat, continually pulling people back and speaking their language when things go out of whack.

Who gets to be a champion? Anyone on the team who has the passion for this particular change and the will to see it through.

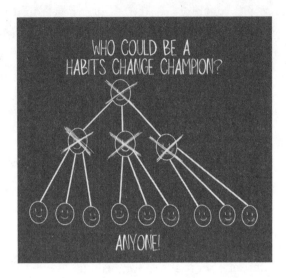

The team champion does not have to be the team leader or manager. In fact, it's a good idea if they are not. First, the existing team managers and leaders already have a lot on their plates. Piling a new change management project onto their to-do stack guarantees that it won't become a priority. Second, nothing about team habit change requires explicit status or power to make it happen. We can make this change together as a team, which means any of us can be the champion for that habit.

The change champion also doesn't have to be the person who is managing the project (although they certainly can be). The advantage of separating the two roles is that it opens the door for people who have the bandwidth to play different roles on the team. The change champion may have the capacity and desire to do the greasing work but not be in a position to manage the project. The person who does have time to manage it may not enjoy taking on the champion work.

The champion can handle the political piece so that the team habit change manager can stay focused on doing the operational work to make things happen. Just be clear about who is taking on each role (even if it is the same person).

It can also be useful to have a champion outside your team in the hierarchy of your organization, especially if the team habit you're changing will have direct implications for other teams. The external champion can explain to people outside the team why you're doing things differently and smooth things over if your new team habits cause conflict with other teams in the organization.

ROCKET PRACTICE

CHOOSE YOUR CHAMPION

» Pick a team habit change champion. For the category of team habit change you are considering, who is best suited to be the champion? If it's not you, why? Is there a need for an external champion outside your team? If so, who would be uniquely suited to that work? Why them?

» Pick a team habit change manager. Who on your team would make an especially good habit change manager? Why them? If not you, why not?

» Before making a final determination about these roles, discuss them with your team. Check to see whether they are aligned, and if so, ask whether there are specific ways in which they can support those players. If not, ask what changes they might like to make and why. Remember, team habit change is about alignment, not power. Do the best you can to incorporate your team's counsel.

» Remember that being a change champion and change manager are both projects and are likely to displace something else those people are doing. As you are discussing these roles with your team, be clear that this will take some focus blocks and may mean that the team members involved will not be fully deployable on other projects.

WHO STANDS TO LOSE?

If identifying the change champion and manager is about specifying who will push this project forward, you also need to identify who will drop an anchor on the project. These are the people who, for whatever reason, are more attached than others to the habit you're trying to change or threatened by the vision you're trying to create.

Someone stands to lose when you start changing things around. It might be the person who is just more resistant to change than others. It might be the person who initiated a change in the past that led to the broken printer you are now trying to fix. It might be the person who is keeping track of your TEAM resources and doesn't want to see those resources diverted from current projects. It might be the teammate who sees your proposed change as one more thing on their plate.

WHAT THE CHAMPION SEES

WHAT THE "LOSER" SEES

A lot of times, it might be the person who is uncertain about what their status and responsibilities will look like after the change. The Goliath of Uncertainty is just as powerful as the Goliath of Inertia. It's human nature to choose the hell we know to avoid dealing with the uncertainty of the heaven we don't know.

When relationships have become comfortable and people have developed mastery around the flow of the current team habits, changing those might cause someone to lose their mastery (remember Bob and his spreadsheets from Part 1?). They might be bumped from the position they enjoy or lose some of the work they like. They're probably not resisting your change in and of itself so much as they're resisting the loss of certainty.

Whatever the reason, your teammate feels that they stand to lose if you start changing things around on this land. How can you respect your teammate's attachment to the way things are while showing that there is a better way to use this land in accordance with their vision (and yours)?

Follow these basic guidelines.

Have Empathy for Your Teammates

Start by assuming that the people you're working with are reasonably competent, mean well, are doing their best, and are fundamentally on your team. This gives you an opening for genuine partnership and generosity that doesn't exist if you start with the assumption that people are idiots and misanthropes.

Extend this empathy both to your immediate teammates and to those outside your team, such as senior leadership.

Get Curious about the Problem

Similarly, instead of assuming that a broken printer needs to be thrown out, start by becoming curious about why it's there in the first place. Why might this thing that—to you—so clearly looks like a problem actually be the most logical response to the current situation?

If the printer always ends up on the third chair in the conference room, why the conference room? Why the third chair? And why don't we get rid of it? One question to spark your imagination here is why a person who has as much intelligence as you (but more perspective on the situation) would make this choice?

Acknowledge the Path That Led Here

Once you learn why something has been happening, acknowledge the positive reasons and decision-making that led to it from a place of respect. This signals to your teammates that you aren't taking a problem out of context but rather trying to work with them to create a solution that works for you all.

This is a matter of subtlety and nuance. It's one thing to say, "I get that you all did it that way, but we're doing it this way now." It's another to say, "I get that we have been really busy and haven't had time to prioritize this because we've been doing the best we can. Now that we have a little bit of space, can we talk about changing this habit?"

Enroll Teammates in a Shared Vision

People don't like being told what to do, especially when you're on their land. Instead of coming in barking directions, use the language of enrollment to invite your teammates into the process of cocreating a shared vision. This makes space for synthesis and creativity, and you might even find that your initial vision becomes richer for inviting others into the process.

When you keep these principles in mind, the path to finding common ground with your teammates becomes fairly clear.

For example, you may have an introverted leader or manager who hates meetings, which is why they tend to keep meetings short and structured. Their goal is just to get to the point and get back to work. When you suggest including a bonding block at the beginning of every meeting to help build team belonging, what your introverted manager hears is that they have to learn how to run meetings in a completely different way. They may like the idea, but in their mind, they lose if they agree.

You could assume they're a stick-in-the-mud who doesn't care if the team bonds. *Or* you could come to them with empathy and curiosity and learn that the reason they run such a rigid meeting is because they simply don't enjoy that part of their job.

When you acknowledge that, it helps you see other options. Instead of asking them to run a new, even more free-form style of meeting, what if you offered to run that block of the meeting? Your introverted manager could still handle the blocks where business happens, but you won't be asking them to take on a big new project. In fact, you'll be taking something off their plate.

SELL THE PROBLEM

When someone is really entrenched, you may need to switch from selling the solution to selling the problem. Think about change in terms of a map. You have your current state, your destination, and your route to get there. Some teammates will be inspired by the destination. Some may become excited about the route. But a handful may not understand why you need to take this road trip in the first place.

If someone is digging in, it's usually a sign that you as the champion haven't explained things well or that they really believe they will lose confidence, mastery, or status if the change occurs. You'll need to tap into every ounce of empathy and curiosity to convince them that it's important to work on the problem. And you'll need to frame the problem using their needs and values rather than your own.

When talking with a teammate, belonging and performance are good places to start. It's hard to argue if you can explain how the problem is negatively impacting team belonging or performance. You can probably agree on what it means to produce high-quality work. If you can agree on that, you can probably agree about the existence of a problem. And if you can agree that you jointly have a problem, you can probably agree that the problem is worth solving with the resources you currently have available.

Maybe you'll still disagree on a certain point of process, but you'll be in alignment that something needs to be done.

When you're dealing with a senior leader who has become the stumbling block, it's still a matter of building an empathetic bridge and speaking on their terms. Be curious about the things that are important to them and learn to convert what you want to do to their language. Will this new habit increase profit? Improve retention and recruiting? Reduce the number of defects or customer complaints? (Hint: The cheat code for getting buy-in from executives on team-level habit change is to find the TIMWOOD waste we talked about in Chapter 8.)

When you figure out what senior leadership cares about and tie your project to that, it becomes hard for them to fight their own priorities. They might disagree about the hows, but you'll be on the same page when it comes to the fact that there's a problem.

Sometimes you might come up against a hard "No" for logistical reasons. Your team is in the middle of a launch, the organization is going through a merger, a critical teammate is on leave. The key question to ask at that point is "I get that we can't do this now. What are the conditions in which we *could* do it?"

Get them to give you a trip wire, such as at the end of this quarter or after the launch. Then build that into your plan and use that time to work on your enrollment. Keep asking your teammates for their input and observing your team's patterns to note places where the new team habit would benefit your team.

You can also work on scaling back the team habit change to a minimum viable change, where the stakes are low enough and the gain is high enough that your team can't help but agree to give it a shot.

It's rarely the case that people will lose as much as they think they will, especially when you have the imagination to cocreate a situation in which their needs and preferences are accommodated. In the end, the question you should ask is not "Did I fix this?" but "Did we solve this problem together?"

ROCKET PRACTICE

BUILD EMPATHY

» Make a map of what each of your teammates stands to lose with your proposed team habit change. (Base these points on the alignment-building conversations you've been having with your teammates rather than making assumptions.) Let's take a look at the example of the introverted manager.

1. Who stands to lose? Alex the manager.

2. What do they stand to lose? Alex feels that in order to lead this new meeting structure, they need to be an extroverted, conversational leader. They'd simply rather not do it.

3. What's the change that solves that need? Alex does not have to facilitate the sections of the meetings that they feel do not resonate with their leadership style.

» As you go through this list, stay curious about why each teammate feels that way. Remember, this is about building alignment, not winning power plays. Think of this list as a tool to help you have cocreative conversations with your teammates about how your proposal and their current state can be complementary—and maybe, just maybe, even better.

» If you are the project champion and not the manager, make sure the manager knows about this list so that they can help ensure that the project is solving people's needs. If any of the references are confidential, please make sure that you have permission to share them. You can also anonymize the responses and share overall themes instead.

» During your reviews for this team habit change project, refer back to this list to ensure that your project is still addressing the different needs and preferences expressed by your teammates. Don't get people to buy in and then completely disregard or fail to address their needs—that's the surest way to corrode trust.

HOW TO ENROLL THE DISENGAGED

We've talked about the people who are for the change and the people who are against it. But what about the people whose response to your proposed team habit change is a shrug emoji?

There are many reasons someone on your team might be disengaged from the project, and most of the time, it has little to do with the change you're proposing itself.

Your teammate might be prochange but not have time to get involved. They may be dealing with change fatigue, especially after a volatile few years of uncertainty. You might not have found their point of alignment yet. Whatever the project is meant to do, it hasn't spoken to things your disengaged teammate cares enough about to get involved.

Or they might legitimately not care one way or the other. It's possible, and quite common, that people just don't have a strong preference. If they're willing to roll with the change, trying to force them to have an opinion can end up creating unnecessary pressure.

Disengagement isn't necessarily a bad thing. First, determine why they're disengaged and the degree to which their disengagement will be a barrier to your project. Next, it's on the champion to figure out what this team member *does* care about in relation to this proposed change.

A simple rocket practice question to ask is "What would get you excited about this project?"

This question works because it doesn't put them on the spot about joining the current project, but it does let you know what types of things they care about as you continue down the path of team habit change. You might also learn some things that you can put on your "Who stands to lose?" map so that you know how to aligned better with them in the future.

Finally, don't take their disengagement as a bad sign. If somebody tells you that they're fine rolling with whatever and happy to play whatever part you give them, trust them. If they say they don't have the bandwidth and time to be involved, trust them. Don't turn their disengagement into a story that derails your work.

Just because someone's disengaged doesn't mean you can completely leave them out of the process, though. Ask if they mind if you keep moving forward with the change and include them in status updates and check-ins. You might find that if you give people space to be intentionally disengaged, they'll start to speak their preferences. Maybe they didn't realize they *had* preferences until you started moving things around. Maybe they didn't realize how excited they'd be by the change until they started experiencing it.

WHAT IF THEY USED TO BE ENGAGED?

What if somebody was previously engaged, but their enthusiasm for the project seems to have died? Most of the time, something happened to cause them to disengage.

Whenever you see a state change from engagement to disengagement, check in with your teammate. But do so from a place of empathy and curiosity rather than assuming that they are now antichange. It could be that your team habit change didn't deliver what it was supposed to or that when you changed the habit, they realized they actually liked things the way they used to be but didn't have a mechanism to tell you that at first. It could also be that they got super busy and are focused on other things or that they have priorities outside work that are soaking up their attention.

It could also be that you're no longer receiving positive feedback because team habits that are working well become invisible. It's hard to forget the broken printer that's causing you so much frustration, but when things are running smoothly, you don't think about them. Sometimes, disengagement can just mean that you succeeded in your habit change and your teammates have moved on to other things, like doing their job without swearing at the printer.

ROCKET PRACTICE

ENROLL YOUR TEAMMATES

» Make space for intentional disengagement to be okay. Remember, disengaged teammates aren't necessarily for or against what you're trying to do. They most likely just don't care. Ask them why they're disengaged and then take them at their word.

» The team habit champion should learn how to express the change in terms of how it will benefit the disengaged teammate. If you're not sure what those ways are, simply ask them what would make them more engaged or what they'd like to see happen—and then listen.

» Remember that a better new normal sometimes goes unappreciated and unspoken. If you as the champion or project manager are not receiving the feedback you would like, don't take it personally. It could just be that your team habit change was a success.

CHAPTER 11 TAKEAWAYS

- Team habit change is about alignment, not power.
- Every team habit change project needs a champion and a project manager (they do not need to be the same person).
- When changing team habits, you're in a fight against the Goliath of Inertia on a teamwide scale. Enroll the help of your teammates by having empathy and understanding what they might stand to lose.
- It's not necessarily a bad thing for your coworkers to be disengaged.

TWELVE

CREATE YOUR TEAM HABIT ROADMAP

We can't control systems or figure them out.
But we can dance with them!

— DONELLA MEADOWS

At this point in the book, you should have chosen a category of team habits that you want to start addressing. The rest of the chapter will discuss how to convert your ideas into a solid plan and will give you the most value if you read it with a specific habit (or category of habits) in mind.

Still not sure where to start? In the chapter on goal-setting, we discussed basic human motivations, including the primal concepts of pain and gain. Asking questions like "What broken printer causes our team the most pain?" or "Where do we have the opportunity to see the biggest gains as a team?" can be an excellent filter to help you choose a first team habit to tackle.

If your team is new to this kind of work, starting with a pain point can give you a tangible win right away. However, be cautious about addressing *only* pain points. We humans are wired very strangely in that we tend to give more weight to pains and discount gains. Most of us are extremely aware of the things that are frustrating us. We deeply feel the incompetence and waste in our workplace—but few of us are aware of the greatness that exists right next to us.

Avoiding pain can make a team more efficient and improve performance and belonging, but if we only ever choose things that make our lives easier (as opposed to things that will create the greatest force for opportunity and gain), these choices will eventually lead to a place of mediocrity and complacency.

START SMALL AND RATCHET UP

Once you have chosen a category to work on, dial in which habits within that category would make the most impact. While it might be tempting to tackle the farthest-reaching habit first, it's more powerful to start small.

It's natural to look at your frustrating meeting culture or feedback culture and want to change the entire thing. But you can't change an entire category at once—it's simply too broad. The good news is that your meeting culture is made up of dozens of discrete yet interlocking habits, and tackling them one at a time will slowly but surely shift the entire meeting culture as a whole.

Take collaboration, for example. Rather than asking the team to work on "collaboration," you can work on the CC Thread from Hell, message bombing in Slack, starting meetings on time, talking about team work in team channels, or any other specific habit with a specific cue that will begin to move the needle.

Give your team an easy win by choosing a team habit change you *know* you can accomplish—something small enough that there's absolutely no reason your team can't pull it off. It could be as simple as getting your team to thread messages in Slack or practice the discipline of writing clear task descriptions in your project management tool. If you're thinking about changing your meeting structure, start by adding or removing one of the building blocks that we talked about in the meeting chapter or making sure that an agenda is sent out before the meeting.

This not only gives your team a small win that can help build momentum but also helps you mitigate the downstream effects that can sometimes happen when we change team habits.

Systems tend to seek equilibrium and stasis. When you change them, they have a way of wanting to revert to their previous state. Systems also often have invisible connections with other activities and systems, which means that if you change one thing, it can have an unforeseen effect somewhere else. Taking five minutes to shout out wins during a meeting displaces other agenda items. Giving someone the green hat requires other teammates to go elsewhere for help that day.

Starting small allows us to see those downstream effects and address them without breaking any one thing. The other advantage of starting small is that it makes it easier to enroll teammates in the change. The funny thing about change is that when you're the initiator, you want to see the biggest impact as quickly as possible. When you are the recipient of a change initiative—even when you agree that it should happen— you probably want change to happen a bit more gradually.

In other words, we want *our* change projects to move quickly, but we want *other* change projects to cause us as little disruption and uncertainty as possible. Navigating this paradox is simply part of team habit change.

If your focus category is meetings, don't start by changing the structure of a meeting whole hog. This can create widespread uncertainty, confusion, and discomfort. But once you lock in that first small behavior (for example, holding five minutes at the end to talk through action items and next steps), next month you can add a meeting block directly before it where everyone on the team shares their meeting highlights.

I want to add one important caveat about starting small and ratcheting up. If any changes are related to people's personal and physical safety, make those changes quickly. If you're working in a plant that has unsafe work practices, those need to be fixed right away.

That said, most of us in knowledge work scenarios aren't in physical danger from our current team habits. We can afford to go slowly and create a sustainable level of team habit change.

PICK YOUR FIRST HABIT

» Brainstorm three to five tiny team habits in your chosen category that you could change. Aim for things that everyone on the team is likely to say yes to and that are small enough to be easy wins.

» Order those changes in a logical sequence. In some cases, one habit will stand out as being foundational for other habits. In a case where any single habit could be the starting point, choose the one that seems likely to create the biggest difference.

» List the "positive" effects that might result from those tiny changes and brainstorm what "negative" downstream consequences might arise so that you can have a plan in place for them.

» Before you lock in the sequence of small changes, run it by at least one teammate to get their sense of things. Remember, the goal is to cocreate these habits and build alignment, not to push your agenda on your teammates.

IT'S A MARATHON, BUT THINK IN SPRINTS

Let's say you decided to start a new running habit on New Year's Day. The first time you hit the pavement, you'll find out very quickly if your old running shoes are shot. It shouldn't take too long to research new shoes and buy them; even if you have to mail-order them, you should be back on your couch-to-5K program pretty quickly.

That same operation becomes considerably harder when you're deciding on shoes for five different people who have different needs. Even the simplest team habit changes can take much longer than expected simply because of the logistics of working with multiple people.

Most likely, getting a team habit change to stick will take many different tries over a long period of time. Very rarely is it a onetime switch, even if it seems like a fairly simple habit to change. That's why when you're planning a team habit change, you need to prepare yourself for a marathon effort of a monthlong or quarterlong project. It takes that long to get everyone on board, cycle through things, and deal with the issues that bubble up along the way.

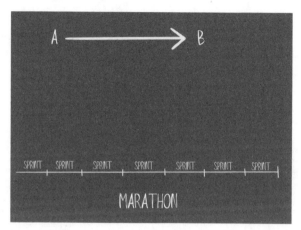

The duration is a marathon, but the many milestones and the expenditure of effort are closer to a sprint in the sense that it will require multiple layers of concerted, focused action to get that habit to stick.

If you think only in terms of sprints, you'll become frustrated by how long it takes to make the change happen. If you think only in terms of marathons, you'll delude yourself about the level of effort required to change entrenched habits.

Let's say you've tweaked your meeting structure. It will take a while before the meeting feels automatic once more. Maybe that first meeting went smoothly, but a teammate was out sick. When they show up at the next meeting, you'll have to explain the new structure and anchor the habit your team is trying to build.

Or, after a few weeks with the new meeting structure, you might realize that the old way you did meetings was a crutch for some other work. Now, because that work hasn't found a home elsewhere, it might rear up and make it super clear that you need to find a way to bring it back into the meeting.

Habit change takes time, and you'll be ahead of the game if you keep that in mind.

Once you create the size of the map or the container you will use (a month or quarter), you can divide the container into sprint segments and start thinking about what should go in each one and what mini-milestones you can check off to mark your journey.

BREAK DOWN YOUR PROJECT

» For the team habit you decide to change, which of the following two time horizons will you use: monthlong or quarterlong? As a general rule, the more mature the organization and the bigger your team, the longer the marathon will take.

» Divide your project into coherent sprints based on your time horizon. If it's a monthlong project, think in weeks. If it's a quarter-long project, think in terms of every-other-week sprint planning.

» Share the general time horizon and sprint planning with your team so that they can provide feedback on the tempo of the project.

HOW WILL YOU TRACK PROGRESS?

How will you know if your change project is going in the right direction? By tracking the pain or gain states that are associated with this changed habit.

For example, the pain from an existing team habit might be that your team is spending an additional two hours a week in crutch meetings to sync everyone with the plan. By improving discipline around communicating updates, you might reduce those extra meetings to one hour a week. Using meeting math, you've freed up five hours of team time—and maybe you've converted that extra time into an additional focus block for every teammate on Thursday mornings.

You decreased the pain (hours spent in meetings) and increased the gain (an additional focus block for everyone).

Or maybe you realize you've been missing opportunities to upsell products or services to customers because no one on the team had visibility of each other's work. Since you've started doing team work in team channels—rather than in side conversations—you've seen an uptick in upsells. You've increased the gain in a tangible way.

When deciding how to track progress on each habit change project, be specific about the current pain or gain states and how you hope to change those over time. Choose tangible goals rather than intangible states such as "excellence." Yes, we want excellence in our teams. But what does that *actually* mean? What is the change state difference between our current state and "becoming more excellent"?

"Excellence" isn't tangible. "Productive" isn't tangible. Cutting the hours our team spent in unnecessary meetings by 50 percent is tangible. Carving out an additional hour per week for every teammate so that they can focus on other work—or maybe even go home a bit earlier—is tangible.

How Will You Report Progress?

As well as tracking progress, you need to report back to your team about how things are going. Tell them the following:

- Here's what we've tried.
- Here's what we've seen happen as it relates to our pain and gain change states.
- Here are some of the unintended consequences of what we are addressing.
- Here's what we're working on next.

You'll notice that the format invites questions, which is why I recommend doing this update as part of a regular meeting rather than sending an update email or posting it in a thread where people will continue discussing it for the next two or three days.

Which meeting your update should be woven into depends on the length of the project. If you are doing a monthlong project, carve out time in the weekly team huddle. If it's a quarterlong project, a monthly update might work just fine. The goal is to find the Goldilocks zone of reporting that keeps your team in the loop and gathers their feedback without soaking up too much time from other work.

A rule of thumb: Carve out five minutes in an existing team meeting structure to give a mini-update and receive feedback about how things are going. If you see that there is a lot of conversation, it might be worthwhile to schedule a separate project-focused meeting where you can use a combination of brainstorming and coworking meeting blocks to dive deeper into tweaking the habit, figuring out what to do with other items that have been shifted around, or fixing things that you might have broken by adding this new team habit.

You're developing a sneaky metahabit here. **When you incorporate conversations about team habit change into your meeting structure, you normalize the fact that you talk about habits and process change.**

This makes talking about other processes and other team habits a lot easier. You don't have to wait until somebody hits a tipping point of pressure or missed opportunities to make a change if you're already in the groove of assessing and improving your team habits.

When you build time into your regular meetings to talk about team habit change, you normalize the fact that you can change your habits for the better and that change doesn't have to happen from the top down. Whatever team habit you're actively working on, you're *also* subtly working on your team's ability to self-improve and increasing your entire team's capacity for leadership.

 **ROCKET PRACTICE**

REPORT ON PROGRESS

» Identify the pain and/or gain states that you expect to shift as you implement the new team habit. Make sure they're things you can measure and track rather than intangible ideas.

» Choose a communication cadence based on how long your project timeline is, and carve five minutes out of the appropriate meeting to update the team on progress. Be prepared to increase the update frequency or schedule an additional meeting if it seems necessary.

EXPECT SETBACKS AND POSITIVE SURPRISES

Every team habit change project will have intended and unintended consequences. Some of these will be frustrating. Some will be exciting. Some will be downright delightful. All can be an opportunity for learning and alignment if you don't turn them into problems.

Knowing setbacks and surprises are coming—and communicating that to your teammates—is the first step in keeping your team habit change project on course. Here are some of the things to be on the lookout for.

It's Not So Easy

That habit you thought would be easy to get your team to rally around turns out to be a hard nut to crack. It could be that the habit is more entrenched than you realized. It could be that shifting team priorities and goals have made it difficult to focus on the habit change. Or maybe a teammate was out for a few weeks, and when they come back, it causes the entire team to collapse back into the original team habit. (Especially if that person is a leader or someone with status on the team who people don't want to call out for doing it the "wrong" way.)

Whatever the reason, you're simply not seeing progress as quickly as you'd like. And that's okay.

Remember, you're trying to change a system, and systems like equilibrium. It might seem simple to add five minutes for nonwork wins to the weekly team huddle, but after two or three meetings, the business stuff that was displaced by that five minutes might start to creep back in. If you're not careful, the new bonding block will be dropped in favor of "more important" agenda items.

Which can really suck, especially if you're the person who felt that they connected with and were seen by their team for the first time. And if you're not the team leader, it can be difficult to speak up and say, "I know that other work is important, but this new thing we've been doing is important, too."

The system naturally re-creates itself, and when it does, it tends to squeeze out the last thing that got added. Part of developing your roadmap is planning how to address that and empowering everyone to speak up.

Downstream Trouble

When you fix one thing in a system, it will inevitably cause something else downstream to become more pronounced. A simple example is rearranging your living room. You might move a chair or a table because it makes more sense for it to be in a different part of the room. But now you notice yourself bumping into something else that the desk or chair was preventing you from bumping into.

A very similar thing happens when you start changing team habits. The team habit you're changing may have kept you from seeing something else that was happening in the team. Once you change it, you expose the sharp point of another habit. That doesn't mean you're doing anything wrong, though.

You're actually doing a lot right because you're exposing your team's habits and operating system. Earlier, I had you brainstorm potential downstream consequences of your proposed team habit change. As you go through this process, keep track of anything that arises that isn't on your list, brainstorm potential solutions, and discuss them with the team during your regular updates.

Once you've been through a few team habit rodeos, you'll have a clearer idea of how your various habit systems interact and become better at anticipating downstream consequences for future projects.

Positive Surprises

Sometimes you move that chair and realize there's a whole new way that you can use the room that you couldn't even see before because the chair was in the way. If you've been working on your meeting habits, you may find that your weekly team meeting ends ten minutes early every time.

What a wonderful surprise! Or maybe because you've been working on your collaboration habits, your teammates aren't as overwhelmed and anxious anymore. Another great surprise!

The funny thing about humans is that we will often discount positive surprises when we come across them. We often won't accept the gift, or we'll be so focused on the things that *aren't* going according to plan that we won't even see it.

Just as you should expect difficulties and downstream effects while doing this work, you should also expect to be positively surprised by outcomes you weren't anticipating.

When you unlock something in the team that you didn't know was there, lean into it and say, "Look what we found together!" Take that gift. Instead of struggling to fill those newly uncovered ten minutes in a meeting, let people go and be free. Instead of anxiously waiting for the other shoe to drop and turn into a Crisco watermelon, remind your team that lowering your collective anxiety is a wonderful surprise to be celebrated.

While it's often true that you'll find positive surprises in business performance outcomes such as increased sales or increased customer satisfaction, the biggest positive surprise I've seen people discover is this: Coming to work just feels better. Even if you can't specifically chart why a team habit change was impactful, you can often see the positive effect it's having on your team day in and day out.

You'll see it in your teammates, too. You might notice a teammate who now shows up to work shining, having unlocked skills none of you would have known were there if you'd kept doing things the way you were. Human talent can shift quickly when it's given space to thrive. Your teammates can rise to the occasion in ways you—and they—could not have imagined before you started making team habit shifts and increasing team belonging and performance.

It's incredible to see a teammate pick up the torch and add their brilliance to it just because you made the space, you let them know how decisions are made, or they had a chance to manage a project. That's where the good stuff is. That's where retention, new capabilities, innovation, and the other standard business results we plan for happen.

HOW TO DEAL WITH SETBACKS AND DOWNSTREAM EFFECTS

If you've done the work with your team to talk about setbacks and downstream effects, it makes it much easier to deal with those issues as they come up. You've already given yourself the conceptual space and emotional permission for things to go off the rails.

Remember that team habit change is a continual process. In most cases, a setback is not fatal to the project—especially if you're starting small. It's a chance to try again, to make your practice better and stronger tomorrow.

Use the meeting reporting structure we talked about earlier to report on setbacks and downstream effects proactively, preemptively, and briefly.

- **Proactive:** Bad news does not get better with time. When things go off the rails, proactively tell somebody about it. If you let them find out on their own, you are likely to trigger a full project inspection when you may not need one.
- **Preemptive:** Be clear about the scope of where the project is off the rails, preempt the questions you know will come up, and give your DRIP for how to go forward.
- **Brief:** Keep your project update succinct. The more you try to mitigate what's going on, the worse you're likely to make your situation. The good thing about being proactive and preemptive is that it affords you the right to be brief. You don't need to go through the whole saga because you're ahead of the situation.

 ROCKET PRACTICE

EXPECT THE UNEXPECTED

» Think back on a change you made in your team that seemed like a setback in the moment but later became a good learning opportunity. Take that as an instruction for how you might share the story of setbacks you run into with your current team habit change process.

» Create some go-to scripts or mantras to use when you are experiencing a setback. It could be something as simple as "OK, this is taking a little bit longer than we hoped, but we are still in the process of making this a habit. We knew delay was a possibility. We just need a little more time." These go-to scripts are helpful in the moment or in a meeting when short-termism and change resistance pop up.

» Think about the last positive surprise that popped up when something changed in your team. How did you approach it? How was it communicated? Looking back, how would you approach it now in a way that really honors the gift that it is?

KNOW WHEN TO HOLD 'EM, FOLD 'EM, OR WALK AWAY

You're prepared for setbacks. But what about complete failures?

Remember, we're starting small here. Much like the unlikely event of the plane crashing in water during an overland flight, the chances of your habit change initiative crashing and burning are pretty small. We're starting off with low stakes, which means the opportunity surface area for complete failure is minimal.

That doesn't mean you won't stall, though. Most of the time, what happens is that you and your team aren't happy with the results, you've reached a point of diminishing returns, or your team simply no longer has the bandwidth to do anything extra. Especially during busy times or in a VUCA environment, one extra ask can break your team's back.

When that happens, listen to Kenny Rogers: You gotta know when to hold 'em, when to fold 'em, and when to walk away.

Hold 'Em

Instead of ratcheting up the small change you started with, hold a steady course and maintain the gains you've made so far.

Maybe the thing that would make your team's life better for the next two to three weeks, all things considered, is to celebrate the broken printer you just solved and run with the work you've done.

A great way to approach this is to say, "We have a lot going on right now. We've made some good progress on our team habit change. We're seeing these benefits, and we've uncovered these things we need to address. For now, let's hold on where we are. We won't go back to the way things were, but we're also not going to keep stacking on new habits right now."

Set a trigger for revisiting the habit change, such as in one month's time or when your team is past the launch or whatever is currently stalling the project. At that point, you can have another conversation and decide whether all is well or whether it's time to reengage.

Even though you thought the team was done with that particular project, if you revisit it, you might find that they're actually happy with the changes. Make the decision on whether to proceed *with* your team rather than *for* them.

Fold 'Em

You might want to fold if you've really examined the situation and seen that whatever you're trying to do is just not working and you need to focus on something else completely. It might be that you realized what you thought was a problem was actually not a problem or that it was a *you* problem rather than a *team* problem.

Maybe the rest of the team has a way of working that doesn't jibe with yours but works well for them. If you've been trying to get the rest of the team to change a perfectly good habit just to benefit your own preference, it might be time to fold.

I want to add a caveat regarding this point. Folks who are from non-dominant cultures or people with disabilities can sometimes be made to feel that the changes they're advocating are *them* problems rather than *team* problems when that really isn't the case. It might be that the rest of your team isn't in a wheelchair, but that doesn't mean they're off the hook for caring about accessibility in the bathroom. Some issues become *team* problems precisely because they affect one member of the team disproportionately.

Walk Away

It might come to a point where you notice that your team's culture and the way the team and the organization want to do things is straight-up incompatible with who you are and the way you want your career to go.

The reality is that not everyone is a perfect fit with every culture. That doesn't necessarily mean there's anything wrong with you, your team, or your organization. But in those circumstances, sometimes the best thing you can do is find your place somewhere else that works better with and for you. At a certain point, if you really do believe in this work but your organization and team do not, your efforts are probably better spent working for an organization that is more philosophically aligned with you.

If you're a leader or manager looking to Sharpie out that sentence before passing this book to the rest of your team, remember that not everyone is the right fit for where you're going.

I recently coached a client through a merger and acquisition. She was worried about team morale because a few team members had left, but when I dug deeper, she admitted that she had known for a while that they weren't good fits. I suggested that if team morale *had* taken a hit, it was because their role hadn't been filled yet, not because that particular person had moved on.

Even the best company or highest-performing team doesn't have a retention rate of 100 percent. And if it does, it probably means it's been accommodating people who aren't the best fit.

That said, **people tend to quit projects and processes far too quickly while staying in situations far too long.**

A team not being open to changing their habits the first few times is not a signal that it's time to walk away or start changing team composition. It may be that the collective ground you're walking on has rich intersubjective meaning that you're still figuring out how to understand and build alignment upon.

ROCKET PRACTICE

NAVIGATE THE STALL

In the unlikely event that your team habit change process is starting to head toward the water, here are some questions to ask.

» Is this a hold 'em scenario? Does the team just need a bit of a breather to focus on other things? Or has your team lost sight of the changes being made and how they are making their work lives better? If you're in a hold 'em scenario, remember that you have not lost, and this is not necessarily a bad thing. Set a time to revisit the question in the future.

» If this is a fold 'em scenario, is the team habit you've been working on more of a you problem than a team problem? Have you picked a team habit that was unexpectedly contentious or entrenched? Going back to your "Who stands to lose" map, can you find another habit that might be easier to build alignment around?

» If this is a walk away scenario, have you given this project or process your best effort? Are you in a place where you're simply not aligned with your team or organization? If so, how do you walk away with integrity in a way that causes the least harm to the team and the organization that you're part of?

HOW TO KNOW WHEN YOU ARE REALLY DONE

When it comes to changing your team's habits, you're never really done. There will always be a place of growth, change, and dynamism within the team.

Teams change, regardless of our efforts. Personnel change. Priorities change. Functional needs change. Change is a constant in life, and every time your team changes, there is potential for your habits to change, too.

Even the most high-performing teams have room for improvement in their team habits. It requires a lot of training, cultivation, and practice to stay at the top of your game.

You'll find that as soon as you're done improving one thing, it opens up many more processes and possibilities for improvement. **With every change, you'll also be training your team in the metahabit of team habit change, creating that positive feedback loop.** When you see it working, you can't help but want to explore the next way you can improve the team. *And the next . . . and the next.*

That said, you can certainly come to a place in your current team habit change project where the amount of effort it will take to continue improving this area—say, collaboration—has reached a point of either diminishing returns or where you're no longer solving the biggest pain or gain point your team is currently dealing with.

If you think of the eight categories of team habits as a wheel or a system, when you poke one, it will create changes in others. When your one habit reaches a place of good enough, another will naturally start to feel like the next place to turn to. And of course, every team habit you change will affect others.

It's a continual process.

You might be reading this while at your desk or in a coffee shop, where it feels like you're sitting still. But you're actually on a planet that's spinning and flying around our sun at about 66,600 mph. This planet is part of a solar system in a galaxy that's also spinning.

In the same way, your role within your team isn't as static as it may seem at any given moment. You're part of a dynamic system that consists of your team, your business unit, your organization, your industry, and the broader society.

When we change our team, we change our organization. When we change our organization, we change the ecosystem our organization operates in. When we make a big enough change in an ecosystem, we start changing the society that we're in. And if COVID-19 has taught us anything, it's that when things change at the environmental level, they reverberate all the way back down to your team.

That's the tension we live in when we do this team habit change work. While we'll never truly be done with the process, we know that at a certain point, it will be time to move on to a new habit.

WHEN TO MOVE ON

» As you approach the end of the time horizon that you set at the beginning of this project, look back to the change state outcomes to track how you've progressed. Are you close to where you thought you'd be? Are there still many rows to hoe? If the latter, do you need to reengage in this team habit category? Or are your time, energy, attention, and money better spent working on another category?

» Keep a log of changes that you've made in your team so you can track the long-term effects of the work you've been doing. Remember, sometimes the more successful you are with a team habit change process, the more likely it is that the work has become invisible. This log shows your team's progress over time and creates a good sense of when you're done with the particular habit you're working on.

» Instead of automatically becoming the champion for the next team habit change process, ask who might be a good cochampion for the next one. After all, changing our team habits is something we *all* can do. And often, the best thing that we can do to help the next person become a great team habit change champion is to invite them in and run beside them.

CHAPTER 12 TAKEAWAYS

- One way to choose which team habit category to start with is to look at which broken printer is giving you the most pain or where you have the most to gain.

- If your team is new to this kind of work, starting with a pain point can give you a tangible win right away.
- Start with a small habit and then ratchet up your team habit change initiative as you gain momentum.
- Team habit change takes time. Plan for project time horizons of a month or quarter and then break that period into sprints.
- Track your progress on the pain or gain state that is associated with your team habit change, and carve five minutes out of an existing team meeting to give teammates regular updates.
- Every team habit change will have unintended consequences: setbacks, downstream effects, and positive surprises. Expect those and plan accordingly.
- If the team habit change starts to stall, evaluate whether it's time to pause, change directions, or walk away entirely.
- Team habit change is a continual process. At some point, it may be time to move to a new habit, but your work to improve your team has limitless potential.

ACKNOWLEDGMENTS

If you ever wonder where my passion and championing for great teams comes from, look no further than the team behind bringing this book to life. With every book I write, I relearn just how much it's a team effort rather than just the work of a single author.

Thanks again to my wonderful agent, David Fugate, for finding a great home for this work with Hachette Go. Thank you to the entire Hachette Go team, but especially Dan Ambrosio, for the decade-long connection and conversations—I'm glad we found a project that was such a great mutual fit.

Two teammates have been and continue to be especially catalytic for this project: Jessie Kwak and Todd Sattersten. Without Jessie's writing, editing, and project management partnership, this book would likely have remained a really good idea without the words to make it a book. Todd's soundboarding, brainstorming, and many rumblings with me during our bookgyms helped polish away a lot of the rough ideas before they even hit the page.

Thank you to Jonathan Fields, Susan Piver, Pam Slim, Jenny Blake, Tara McMullin, Noah Brockman, and Larry Robertson for all the feedback, encouragement, commiseration, and belief that kept me in the mix of this project. They knew what felt impossible to me at the time was just another leg of the journey that I'd find my way through.

Thank you to Team PF—Shannon McDonough, Josephine Cherry, Jess Sommers, Steve Arensberg, Osheyana Martinez, Maghan Haggerty, Cory Huff, Mary Clare Oliver, Nicole Chaplin, Julianna Young, Michael Prather, Mariah Williamson, and our bonus Magical Team led by Christina Salerno and Olivia Wirick. Your participation in great team habits and patience to try new habits have infused this book.

Thank you to Jill Boots, Mallory Corlette, Rex Williams, John Nicholson, Alli Blum, Jenn Labin, Nicole Jennings, Leslie Robertson, Liana Cassar, Mike Bruny, Patricia Bravo, Jenny Blake, Jeremie Miller, Kate Strathmann, Kendra Bork, and some of the souls above who gave constructive feedback and suggestions on an early version of the manuscript.

Thank you to the Productive Flourishing community members and clients who have supported this work from the beginning. Without your stories, questions, nudges, and encouragement, this and little else of my work would exist.

And my wife, Angela Wheeler, continues to be both an anchor and catalytic force for everything I do. She was the champion for this book when it was a placeholder idea in 2013 and continues to be so every step along the way. ILYB&WB.

RECOMMENDED READING

The books that follow are excellent next reads, either because they take the main theme of the chapter deeper or provide additional rocket practice suggestions. I'll be sharing short summaries of the books on this list and keeping the list updated at http://www.teamhabitsbook.com/resources.

CHAPTER 1: WE NEED BETTER TEAM HABITS NOW MORE THAN EVER

Antifragile by Nassim Nicholas Taleb
The Future is Faster Than You Think by Steven Kotler
Thinking in Systems by Donella Meadows

CHAPTER 2: WE LIVE AND BREATHE TEAM HABITS

Atomic Habits by James Clear
The Five Dysfunctions of a Team by Patrick Lencioni
The Progress Principle by Teresa Amabile, Steven Kramer, et al.

CHAPTER 3: BELONGING

Belonging: The Science of Creating Connection and Bridging Divides by Geoffrey Cohen
Design for Belonging by Susie Wise
The Power of Emotions At Work by Karen McLaren
Sparked by Jonathan Fields

CHAPTER 4: DECISION-MAKING

Decisive by Chip and Dan Heath
Free Time by Jenny Blake
Radical Alignment by Alexandra Jamieson and Bob Gower
Subtract by Leidy Klotz

CHAPTER 5: GOAL-SETTING AND PRIORITIZATION

4 Disciplines of Execution by Chris McChesney, Sean Covey, et al.
Objectives and Key Results by Paul R. Niven and Ben Lamorte
What Works by Tara McMullin

CHAPTER 6: PLANNING

12 Week Year by Brian P. Moran and Michael Lennington
Project Management for Humans by Brett Harned
Start Finishing by Charlie Gilkey

CHAPTER 7: COMMUNICATION

Fierce Conversations by Susan Scott
Radical Candor by Kim Scott
Turn This Ship Around by L. David Marquet

CHAPTER 8: COLLABORATION

The 24-Hour Rule by Adrienne Bellehumeur
The Coaching Habit by Michael Bungay Stanier
Six Thinking Hats by Edward de Bono

CHAPTER 9: MEETINGS

HBR Guide to Making Every Meeting Matter by Harvard Business Review
Leading Great Meetings by Richard M. Lent, PhD
Read This Before Our Next Meeting by Al Pittampalli

CHAPTER 10: CORE TEAM HABITS

Deep Work by Cal Newport
The Gift of Struggle by Bobby Herrera
The Power of When by Michael Breus, PhD
Tranquility by Tuesday by Laura Vanderkam

CHAPTER 11: TEAM HABITS ARE POLITICAL—SO PLAY THE GAME

Emergent Strategy by Adrienne Maree Brown
The Insider's Guide to Culture Change by Siobhan McHale
When Everyone Leads by Ed O'Malley and Julia Fabris McBride

CHAPTER 12: CREATE YOUR TEAM HABIT ROADMAP

Courageous Cultures by Karin Hurt and David Dye
Little Bets by Peter Sims
Managing Transitions, 3rd Edition, by William Bridges, Lloyd James, et al.
Our Iceberg Is Melting by John Kotter and Holger Rathgeber

GLOSSARY

3x Rule: Assume that strategic work will be three times more intensive than you initially thought.

85 Percent Rule: Your team's capacity should only ever be filled to 85 percent.

After-Action Review: A review of a previous project or activity to see what worked and what didn't work and to bring insights that you can apply to current or future plans and projects to the surface.

Air Sandwich: The often missing planning step between setting a goal and executing it.

Atomic Element: The minimum doer-reviewer-coordinator functions that need to exist within a team.

Bread Crumbs: Documentation around a project or task that allows others (or your future self) to see where you left off and your plans for going forward.

Broken Printers: Shorthand for all those small and fixable breaks in the ways we work with each other.

Bumps: The accidental ways in which we introduce friction into the relationship with our teammates.

CC Thread from Hell: The practice of CCing a new person on a long-running email thread with no additional context, requiring them to scroll back through the entire email conversation to decipher what information is important or what action is needed. Other uses may include CCing everyone without regard or consideration for who actually needs to know.

Chronotype: Your personal natural rhythm: morning larks, afternoon emus, and night owls.

Commit:Complete Ratio: For every project you commit to, how many do you complete?

Crisco Watermelons: The missed handoffs and dropped balls that occur when teams collaborate on projects.

Crutch Meetings: Meetings that act as stand-ins for poor team habits. Crutch meetings often address things that should have been taken care of outside the meeting.

DRIP: Shortcode for "decision, recommendation, intention, or plan," used to indicate the user's intention for next steps.

Dunkirk Spirit: The pattern in which, despite terrible planning and decision-making, a team rallies and accomplishes a daunting goal through valiant efforts, long hours, and sheer tenacity.

Five Projects Rule: You should have no more than five active projects per time scale (year, quarter, month, week, or day).

Five-Sentences Rule: Limit all email responses to five sentences or fewer.

Focus Block: Those ninety-minute to two-hour blocks of time in which we can do deep work and stay focused enough on a project to move it forward or complete it.

Ghost Plan: A plan that was made by a few members of the team but not communicated to the rest of the team.

Goldilocks Zone: A reference to the "just right" middle bowl of porridge from the fairy tale, "Goldilocks and the Three Bears." In the context of teams, it's finding the middle option that satisfies the conditions without over-producing or under-producing work to get there; rarely is there a perfect solution that satisfies all considerations.

Green Hat: The person with the green hat currently owns the main effort for pushing a project forward and should be given priority to focus on that work until they've finished it.

IKEA Effect: The cognitive bias where people tend to place a high value on outcomes, products, and experiences they have partially created.

Meeting Math: A calculation of the true cost of meetings in terms of actual hours and salary spent.

One-Third–Two-Thirds Rule: Only one-third of the time allocated to execute a plan should be spent creating the plan, and two-thirds should be left to complete the project.

Project Cage Match: The process of eliminating the weakest projects in order to keep your team's priorities under the Five Projects Rule.

Readiness: The capability of a team or individual to accomplish their goals, complete their projects, and perform to standard.

Shortcodes: The acronyms and unique phrases your team uses to communicate rich information in only a few letters or words.

Strategic-Routine-Urgent Logjam: When accomplishing urgent and routine work regularly becomes the biggest priority, and strategic work falls by the wayside.

Team: A group that's highly aligned, where the members feel a sense of belonging and a shared sense of purpose. In this book, it usually refers to the four to eight people who we interact with daily or multiple times per week.

Team Habits: A subset of workways; how we work together in a team.

TIMWOOD: A framework to help identify the common sources of waste in your team or organization: transportation, inventory, motion, wait time, overproduction, overprocessing, and defects.

VUCA Environment: An environment that is volatile, uncertain, complex, and ambiguous.

Wolf: The person (whether an internal or external expert) who you call to handle a particular problem whenever it arises.

Workways: How we work with each other, determined by a mix of our team habits, organizational policies, technology, regulatory compliance, and org structure.

NOTES

CHAPTER ONE

1. Steven Kramer and Teresa Amabile, *The Progress Principle: Using Small Wins to Ignite Joy, Engagement, and Creativity at Work* (Harvard Business Press, 2011).

2. Marcus Chiu and Heather Salerno, *Changing Change Management: An Open Source Approach* (Gartner, 2019).

3. Nassim Nicholas Taleb, *Skin in the Game: Hidden Asymmetries in Daily Life* (Random House, 2018).

4. *The Definitive Guide to Peer Coaching* (Imperative, 2019).

5. William G. Robertson, *Case Studies from the Long War*, vol. 1 (Combat Studies Institute Press, 2006), https://apps.dtic.mil/sti/pdfs/ADA462790.pdf.

6. Kim Scott, *Radical Candor: Be a Kick-Ass Boss without Losing Your Humanity* (St. Martin's Press, 2019).

CHAPTER TWO

1. Charlie Gilkey, *Start Finishing: How to Go from Idea to Done* (Sounds True, 2019).

2. Douglas Conant and Mette Norgaard, *Touchpoints: Creating Powerful Leadership Connections in the Smallest of Moments* (Jossey-Bass, 2011).

CHAPTER THREE

1. Howard Behar, *It's Not about the Coffee: Lessons on Putting People First from a Life at Starbucks* (Portfolio, 2007).

2. Priya Parker, *The Art of Gathering: How We Meet and Why It Matters* (Riverhead Books, 2018).

CHAPTER FOUR

1. David Marquet, *Turn the Ship Around! How to Create Leadership at Every Level* (Greenleaf Book Group Press, 2012).
2. William Oncken, Jr., and Donald L. Wass, "Management Time: Who's Got the Monkey?," *Harvard Business Review* (1974).

CHAPTER FIVE

1. Daniel H. Pink, *Drive: The Surprising Truth about What Motivates Us* (Riverhead Books, 2011).
2. Seth Godin, *Leap First: Creating Work That Matters* (Sounds True, 2015).
3. Gary Hamel and C. K. Prahalad, *Competing for the Future* (Harvard Business Review Press, 1996).

CHAPTER SIX

1. "Gnomes," *South Park*, created by Trey Parker and Mat Stone, season 2, episode 17 (Comedy Central, December 16, 1998).
2. Leidy Klotz, *Subtract: The Untapped Science of Less* (Flatiron Books, 2021).
3. Edward de Bono, *Six Thinking Hats* (Little, Brown and Company, 1985).
4. Michael Porter, "What Is Strategy?," *Harvard Business Review* (November–December 1996).

CHAPTER SEVEN

1. Todd Sattersten, "The New World of Book Publishing" in-person speech, Portland, Oregon (2012).
2. Jason Fried, Twitter (January 2, 2020, 12:03 p.m.), https://twitter.com/jasonfried/status/1212826719561891841.

CHAPTER EIGHT

1. Bud Abbott and Lou Costello, "Who's on First," *Hollywood Bandwagon* (1937).
2. Tomoko Yokoi and Jennifer Jordan, "Using Emojis to Connect with Your Team," *Harvard Business Review* (May 2022).

CHAPTER NINE

1. Fred Reichheld, *The Ultimate Question: Driving Good Profits and True Growth* (Harvard Business School Press, 2006).

CHAPTER TEN

1. Daniel H. Pink, *When: The Scientific Secrets of Perfect Timing* (Riverhead Books, 2018).

2. Michael Breus, *The Power of When: Discover Your Chronotype—and Learn the Best Time to Eat Lunch, Ask for a Raise, Have Sex, Write a Novel, Take Your Meds, and More* (Little, Brown Spark, 2019).

INDEX